ARNOUL GRÉBAN

The Mystery of the Passion
The Third Day

PEGASUS
PRESS

ARNOUL GRÉBAN

The Mystery of the Passion
The Third Day

Translated by Paula Giuliano

Early European Drama Translation Series

Martin Stevens and *Stephen K. Wright*, General Editors

pegasus press
University of North Carolina
Asheville, North Carolina
1996

Library of Congress Cataloging-in-Publication Data

Gréban, Arnoul, ca. 1420–1471.
  [Mistère de la Passion. 3. journée. English]
  The mystery of the Passion. The third day / by Arnoul Gréban;
translated by Paula Giuliano.
        p. cm. — (Early European drama translation series)
  Includes bibliographical references and index.
  ISBN 1–889818–01–1
  1. Jesus Christ—Passion—Drama. 2. Mysteries and miracle-
plays, French—Translations into English.   3. Passion-plays—
Translations into English. I. Giuliano, Paula, 1962– . II. Title.
III. Series.
  PQ1357.P2G813 1995
  842 '.2—dc20   94–48936
                                                                  CIP

This book was edited and produced
by MRTS at SUNY Binghamton.
This book is made to last.
It is set in Palatino, smyth-sewn,
and printed on acid-free paper
to library specifications.

Printed in the United States of America

The Early European Drama Translation Series

The Early European Drama Translation Series is a project established under the auspices of the Medieval and Renaissance Drama Society. The purpose of the EEDT series is to provide reliable, inexpensive translations of major European vernacular plays from the Middle Ages and Renaissance for use in a wide variety of undergraduate and graduate courses. It is the explicit intent of the series to internationalize the teaching and study of the early theater by supplying translations of important texts from many genres: mystery plays, saint plays, history plays, miracles, moralities, folk plays, carnival plays, processionals, and civic and ecclesiastical ceremonies of every kind.

The General Editors of the EEDT series are Martin Stevens and Stephen K. Wright. Members of the Advisory Board include Kathleen Ashley, Konrad Eisenbichler, Kathleen Falvey, Gordon Kipling, Alan E. Knight, Robert Potter, and Eckehard Simon.

Contents

Acknowledgements

This book could not have been written without the help of others who have generously shared their time and knowledge. Martin Stevens, under whose guidance I have developed as a scholar, first suggested this project and oversaw it to its completion. From Frederick Goldin, who is an inspirational teacher and translator, I have learned the difficult pleasure of translation. Through their careful editorial work, Alan E. Knight and Stephen K. Wright have helped shape the book into its final form. I offer sincere thanks to all who have contributed to this book, which I dedicate to my parents and to my husband.

Introduction

ARNOUL GRÉBAN AND THE FRENCH PASSION PLAY

The earliest surviving Passion play written in French, *La Passion du Palatinus*, dates from the first half of the fourteenth century. Like other early Passions, it is based on the so-called *Passion des Jongleurs*, a narrative poem covering the events of Holy Week.[1] By way of contrast, most fifteenth-century Passion plays greatly expand their scope and dramatize almost all episodes of Christ's life as recounted by the evangelists and the apocryphal gospels. The three great Passions of fifteenth-century France were composed by Eustache Marcadé, Arnoul Gréban, and Jean Michel, each of whom influenced his successor.

Eustache Marcadé's drama, *La Passion d'Arras*, dating from approximately the first quarter of the fifteenth century, differs considerably from both earlier and contemporary Passion plays. Length alone accounts for most of the differences—Marcadé's play exceeds the others by at least 15,000 lines, the next longest play being *La Passion de Semur*, which contains 10,000 lines and dates from roughly the same period. Obviously, then, Marcadé adds much greater detail when dramatizing the same scenes as other playwrights, but he also creates entirely new episodes. Two other important changes first appear in his work. He divides his drama into four Days (*journées*) centering on Christ's Infancy, Ministry, Passion, and Resurrection.[2] He also frames the play with the Trial in Paradise in which the Four Daughters of God (Mercy, Justice, Wisdom, and Truth) debate whether and how humankind

---

[1] Another early play, *La Passion d'Autun*, is also based on *La Passion des Jongleurs*.

[2] Each Day delineates a distinct stage in Christ's life and does not necessarily correspond to an actual day's performance.

should be redeemed. Although Marcadé's drama contains many distinct features, we have no way of knowing whether he originated them or borrowed them from other lost plays.

Arnoul Gréban's *Mystère de la Passion*, which runs to approximately 35,000 lines, follows Marcadé's general outline but is 10,000 lines longer. Gréban greatly improves on Marcadé's play by carefully interweaving scenes, making events causally linked to one another, individuating characters through their use of speech, and offering coherence by focusing on man's need for salvation. Though both dramatists write in octosyllabic couplets, the standard verse form in French Passions, Gréban has a much greater poetic range. Omer Jodogne, his most recent editor, counts twenty different verse forms including rondeaux, virelais, fatras, tercets, and quatrains. Gréban's characters also reflect a wide variety of diction ranging from contemporary Parisian idioms to highly stylized academic debate to lyrical pathos. Gréban was both an outstanding dramatist and poet. That his play enjoyed a huge success is demonstrated by its survival in many manuscripts, its frequent performances, and its influence on other Passion plays.

BIOGRAPHY

Arnoul Gréban was born around 1420. In 1450 he became assistant to the boys' choirmaster at Notre Dame de Paris where he already was an organist. He was promoted to master of the choirboys in 1451 and resigned from this position in 1455.

Gréban attended the University of Paris where he studied theology. In 1456 he is listed as registering for a course with Thomas of Courcelles, a dean at Notre Dame. Gréban is here given the title of *magister*. According to a rubric in Manuscript A of his *Passion*, Gréban later held a bachelor's degree in theology. This same rubric also indicates that he wrote his play at the request of some people in Paris. Another document states that the town of Abbeville paid him 10 gold *écus* in 1452 for a copy of his play, so that we know that he wrote it some time before this date, perhaps while serving as organist or assistant choirmaster.

After 1456 there are no more records concerning Arnoul Gréban. Pierre Champion, who has given the fullest, if somewhat fanciful, account of Gréban's life, surmises that he later left for Le Mans where his brother Simon was a canon. Simon Gréban also wrote a play, *Les Actes des Apôtres (The Acts of the Apostles)*, and because scholars long thought that the two brothers had collaborated on it, Arnoul Gréban has often been associated with Le Mans.[3] Champion's belief is also partially

---

[3] Lacroix du Maine in his history of French literature, *Bibliothèque françoise*

based on the fact that in 1455 Arnoul Gréban asked for a month's leave from the duties of choirmaster in order to visit Charles of Anjou, the Count of Maine. Champion believes that the Count later found a position for Arnoul in Le Mans, the capital of Maine.

MANUSCRIPTS

Arnoul Gréban's *Passion* survives in nine whole and partial manuscripts, an enormous number given that most medieval dramatic texts exist in only a single copy.[4] Another unusual feature is that in comparison with other plays, there are comparatively few variants among the manuscripts, all of which date from the fifteenth and sixteenth centuries. Two manuscripts (known to modern editors as A and B) preserve the entire play, including a 1,740-line Prologue dramatizing Old Testament material, and another two manuscripts (C and D) contain all four Days[5]. The remaining six manuscripts (E,F,G,H,I and J) are fragmentary, preserving from as much as three Days to as little as 3,000 lines of the play.[6] These manuscripts, with the possible exception of Manuscript G which contains elaborate musical and staging directions, were presentation or luxury copies meant for reading. Manuscripts A and B (both of which were specifically commissioned works) and Manuscript C all contain many miniatures depicting characters and events from the text.

The two manuscripts that preserve the entire play have each served as a base text for the two separate modern editions of Gréban's *Passion*. For their 1878 edition, Gaston Paris and Gaston Raynaud used Manuscript A, dated by its copyist as being completed in 1472 (1473 according to our calendar). They regard it as the oldest manuscript.

(1584), states that Simon Gréban continued *Les Actes des Apostres* begun by Arnoul. *The Acts of the Apostles* remains unedited.

[4] Gréban's Fourth Day was also attached to Jean Michel's *Passion* in five early printed editions.

[5] Modern designations for the surviving manuscripts of Gréban's play are as follows: **A** (Paris, Bibl. Nat. f fr. 816); **B** (Paris, Bibl. Nat. f. fr. 815); **C** (Paris, Arsenal 6431); **D** (Rome, Accademia dei Lincei, Ms. Corsini col. 44 A 7); **E** (Chantilly, Musée Condé 614); **F** (Paris, Bibl. Nat. f. fr. 15064–15065); **G** (Le Mans, Bibl. Municipale, no. 6); **H** (Paris, Bibl. Nat. f. fr. 1550); **I** (Paris, Bibl. Nat. Nouvelles Acquisitions françaises 14043); **J** (Paris, Bibl. Nat. Nouvelles Acquisitions françaises 12908). For complete descriptions, see Jodogne, II, 11–13.

[6] They consist of respectively the first three Days (Manuscript E), the Prologue and the first two Days (Manuscript F), the First Day (Manuscript G), the Prologue and the First Day (Manuscript H), and 3,000 lines from the nativity in the First Day. Graham Runnalls convincingly argues that fragments I and J originally belonged to the same manuscript in, "Quatre fragments de mystères de la Passion," *Miscellanea Gasca Quinazza* 2 (1988): 911–18.

Omer Jodogne, believing Manuscript B to be from 1458 and hence older than A, used it as the base text for his 1965 edition. This edition was followed in 1983 by a supplemental volume containing such textual apparatus as the variants in all manuscripts, a listing of all rhymes and their appearances, a glossary, and copious linguistic observations supporting Jodogne's dating of Manuscript B.[7] Jodogne's edition serves as the text for this translation.

SOURCES

In constructing his vast drama, Gréban naturally enough turns to all four evangelists and the apocryphal gospels, thus accumulating a great wealth of detail. He borrows mainly from Matthew and Luke, who offer the greatest number of episodes easily adaptable for dramatization.[8] Gréban also borrows from John, especially in recounting the Passion.

Although Gréban is a highly original and skillful dramatist, he generally follows the overall dramatic structure of Marcadé's *Passion d'Arras*. Some scholars like Émile Roy, who has done the most thorough study to date of Gréban's sources, believe that Gréban closely read Marcadé's play. Émile Roy extracts certain scenes common to both plays and offers these as proof of his argument. Some of the more unusual ones like the origin of the wood of the cross, the legend of Saint Dionysus, and Satan's explanation of the points on a die certainly seem to indicate a close knowledge of Marcadé's play, since they are not dramatized in previous French Passions. However, they do not offer proof that Gréban read Marcadé's play; he could easily have remembered such episodes if he had seen them performed, especially since they are part of traditional Christian lore. The first two, for example, are also found in the *Legenda Aurea* (*The Golden Legend*), which does serve as a source for Gréban. Finally, then, we can be sure that Gréban knew Marcadé's work, but both the extent and the means of his familiarity with it remain uncertain.

Émile Roy traces Gréban's other sources, the second most important being the *Postillae* of Nicholas of Lyra, a Franciscan exegete who wrote a commentary on the Gospels between 1322 and 1330. Some of the quotations Roy cites as evidence of the influence of Nicholas of Lyra on Gréban are not completely convincing. For example, when the

---

[7] For two reviews which support the choice of Jodogne's edition as the definitive text, see Gilles Roques, *Revue de Linguistique Romane*, 47 (1983), 511–14, and Pierre Ruelle, *Romania*, 104 (1983), 589–91.

[8] Because Mark's rather bare narrative contains little not found in the other two synoptic gospels, Gréban only occasionally uses it.

Centurion makes the simple observation that the blood and water flowing from Christ's side signify a mystery, Gréban does not necessarily refer to the elaborate symbolism developed by Nicholas of Lyra, who explains that the water is for the washing of sins and that it proves Christ was composed of the four elements (Roy, 233). Other passages, however, do show a close association. For example, both Nicholas of Lyra and Gréban explain that the Jews dress Christ in his own clothes for the march to Calvary so that he may be more easily recognized (Roy, 230).

Other sources Gréban borrows from are the *Legenda Aurea*, the *Meditationes Vitae Christi (Meditations on the Life of Christ)*, The Gospel of Nicodemus, the *Summa Theologica* of Aquinas (the title of which is specifically cited in the First Day), and the *Passion Isabeau* (Roy, 207).[9] The first three are frequently used by other medieval dramatists as well. All references to Gréban's sources are indicated in the notes to the translation.

PERFORMANCE HISTORY

Whether performed on its own or incorporated into a new text, Arnoul Gréban's *Passion* was an enormously successful and influential play. It was performed in Paris three times before 1473 (Jodogne, 10) and, as already noted, the city of Abbeville paid ten gold *écus* for a copy of the play (Paris and Raynaud, ii). It formed the basis of a production mounted in Troyes every year from 1482 to 1490 and again in 1496, 1505, and 1531. The *Passion de Troyes* (23,098 lines) borrows from the First, Second, and Fourth Days of Gréban's play; the section dramatizing the Passion itself is missing from the Troyes manuscript. About one fourth of the *Passion de Troyes* (5,940 lines) is original or greatly altered material, while the remaining three fourths of the text was directly copied from Gréban (Bibolet, xi–xviii).

The most important play influenced by Gréban is Jean Michel's *Passion*, which, benefitting from the invention of the printing press, went through seventeen editions between circa 1487 and 1550. It was edited again in 1959 by Omer Jodogne. Michel's play, beginning with the sermon of St. John the Baptist (as does Gréban's Second Day) and ending with the Crucifixion, runs to about 30,000 lines. Jean Michel directly copies about 65% of Gréban's Second and Third Days, but these

---

[9] The *Passion Isabeau* has been edited for the first time by Edelgard DuBruck (New York: Peter Lang, 1990). She examines this Passion's influence on Gréban and other authors in "The *Passion Isabeau* and Its Relationship to Fifteenth Century *mystères de la passion*," *Romania*, 107 (1986), 77–91. Phrases that Gréban has in common with the *Passion Isabeau* but that are lacking in the *Passion d'Arras* are indicated in the notes to the translation.

borrowings make up a total of 38% of Michel's work; the rest is original. The percentage, however, increases in Michel's Fourth Day, 58% of which is copied from Gréban's Third Day (Jodogne, xxxvii).

The two plays were often combined to serve as the text for a performance as in the case of the *Passion* produced in Mons in 1501, for which we have highly detailed records. The city of Amiens must have had the same script since the Montois copied its text (Cohen, 474). A famous twenty-five day *Passion* performed in Valenciennes in 1547 also combined both texts (Petit de Julleville, II, 422).

In total, we have records of seventeen productions for which Gréban's drama provided the whole or a substantial part of the script. These seventeen performances took place in many cities throughout northern France and were produced over a period of nearly one hundred years. If we consider the immense effort, time, and money involved in staging a production of this size, the number of performances becomes even more impressive. Certainly no other medieval French Passion play can claim such success or longevity.

Gréban's *Passion* has also attracted modern audiences. In 1935 it was performed in a greatly abridged version before the steps of Notre Dame in Paris to a crowd of twelve thousand. In 1950 Gustave Cohen wrote an adaptation of the Passions of Gréban and Michel and performed it with an acting troupe from the Sorbonne in Rouen, Brussels, and Paris. In 1961 the BBC had James Kirkup translate and adapt the play for radio and television. Translations intended for a reading audience have also been recently published. Micheline de Combarieu du Grès and Jean Subrenat have translated parts of all four days into modern French, omitting some ten thousand lines, and Shelley Sewall has translated the Nativity episodes into English.

THE STAGING OF THE MONS *PASSION* IN 1501

Since few records of specific medieval theatrical performances still exist, the survival of a full production record of the Gréban-Michel *Passion* at Mons from 5–12 July 1501 is of special interest to students of early drama. A record of the expenses for this production and a director's handbook, including numerous stage directions and the first and last lines of each character's speeches, were edited by Gustave Cohen in *Le livre de conduite du régisseur et le compte des dépenses pour le mystère de la Passion joué à Mons en 1501* (*The Director's Handbook and the Expense Record for the Mystery of the Passion Performed at Mons in 1501*).

The staging of the Mons *Passion* was a spectacular event, part of a great celebration filled with festivities of all sorts.[10] In the evening

---

[10] A procession, probably consisting of important clerical and secular person-

after each day's performance more entertainment was offered, including shorter plays, other amusements like singing or acrobatics, and a contest featuring the recitation of poetry.

Letters announcing the festival were sent to some thirty towns including Valenciennes, Arras, Amiens, Cambrai, Tournai, Lille, and Douai. The Princess of Castile expressed an interest in attending, although she was unable to do so. The Bishop of Cordoba, however, did attend and was given a feast at the town's expense. The audience ranged from approximately 2,500 to 6,300 people, with the first and the last days (a Monday and a Sunday respectively) drawing the largest crowds.[11] Most tickets cost twelve *deniers* or about one eighth of an artisan's average daily wage as listed in the expense accounts. Benches were provided for sitting, but wealthier spectators sat on specially built scaffolding which afforded a better view and cost three *sous* or triple the entrance fee of twelve *deniers*.

Lack of precise terminology for the stage, scaffolding, and the theater as a whole, which were all called *hourt* (Rey-Flaud, 190), and the lack of configurations for the stage and audience space make the performance area difficult to reconstruct. The stage, located in the Great Market or plaza, was aligned against a row of houses. One of these, *la Maison d'Allemaigne*, was actually incorporated into the scenery since it contained the machinery that lowered a cloud used in the Great Flood episode (Cohen, 561). From this entry and another mentioning "L'entrée du Hour envers le Seuwe" (the stage entrance near the Seuwe [another house]), Cohen (xlvi) estimates the length of the stage at about forty meters.[12] The scaffolding that provided the expensive seating was built close to the row of houses facing the stage. Stakes or posts were planted to form the theatrical enclosure. They probably ran in two lines perpendicular to the houses, thus forming a closed-off square within the larger plaza and allowing the stage to be viewed from three sides.[13]

---

ages, preceded the first day's performance and established a religious atmosphere, since the consecrated host was usually prominently displayed in such processions.

[11] These figures are calculated by dividing the total receipts of one day by the price of the cheapest and most popular ticket costing 12 *deniers*. These figures are only approximate because there is no way of knowing precisely how many tickets were bought at the more expensive price of 3 *sous*.

[12] The problem with this estimate is that Cohen, as Rey-Flaud points out in *Le Cercle magique* (195), arbitrarily fixes the end of the stage at another house, the *maison* Franeau. The stage, however, had to be quite large to accommodate the many simultaneous sets.

[13] Cohen interprets the entry, "A Pierart de Lattre, pour II jours par lui employés *à planter les estacques de le cloture dudit Hourt*," (To Pierart de Lattre for

The stage, crowded with various sets and exploding with color, was a spectacular setting for some 150 actors playing approximately 350 characters (Cohen, cvii). The accounts record the purchase of gold and silver leaf, vermillion, black, yellow (517), indigo (532), and brown (544). We can assume that they were used to paint scenery even though the records do not specify their use. The producers brought trees with real cherries and apples attached to them, rabbits, pigeons, sheep, and even live fish (564), an ass for Mary, and a small boat for the apostles (533). Devils exited in a puff of smoke (199), and Christ disappeared through a trap-door (413) and rose through the air when ascending to Heaven (449).

The most eye-catching set, one requiring enormous ingenuity and labor, was Hell. Three men took a total of eleven days (498, 519, 528) and seventeen cartloads of clay (505, 534) to plaster (*placquier*) and then paint Hell (499). They probably covered over some kind of structure resembling a fortress, a common representation of Hell in medieval art. It had two doors (513) that shook at Jesus' arrival in Limbo (383), and from it or near it hung the Hell Mouth, here called "la gheule du Crapault d'Enffer" (the mouth of the Hell Toad [507]).[14] Cohen places Hell at stage left, opposite Paradise, while Rey-Flaud believes that it faced the stage and was built on its own scaffolding near the one for expensive seating.

Somewhere on top of Hell there was either an actor or a dummy representing the devil. Other embellishments were a dragon's head and a snake's head (486), serpents made of wicker (505, 516), and serpents made of iron tubing through which flames were shot (498). Human limbs also made of wicker were arranged to represent the torture of the damned.

The most terrifying features of Hell were its thunder and fire. The first was produced easily enough, with copper basins (583) or empty vats, probably filled with stones as Cohen surmises (514). This racket was compounded by explosives (536) and fire-throwing machines (531), of which there were at least ten. Hell's machinery was operated by seventeen men. All the equipment and figures were protected by a

---

the two days used by him to plant the stakes around the said stage. [The italics are Cohen's]) as signifying that the stage was open only on the side facing the spectators (519). In interpreting *hourt* to mean stage, Cohen forms a conclusion that is not very plausible. If the stage could be viewed from only one side by those on ground level, then the audience would be impossibly packed into the area directly facing the stage.

[14] Hell Mouth was typically represented by the head of a monstrous animal with gaping jaws through which actors enter or exit Hell.

tent when the stage was not in use (501), and people were hired to guard the stage at night.

Less awesome than Hell was Paradise, whose structure is not as clearly described. Stage directions like "Lors Dieu et ses angles s'en revienent desoubz Paradis" (Then God and his angels return underneath Paradise), "Lors Dieu et ses angles s'en revont en Paradis et plus ne desc[h]end Dieu" (Then God and his angels return to Paradise and God no longer descends), and "Soit (cy) adverti le secret pour faire eslever Jhesus" (Let the machinery that elevates Christ be prepared here) indicate that Paradise had two levels, both of which were used as performance spaces. On the upper level various *secrets* (stage effects) were also manipulated and stored. For example, an empty wine barrel which was used in the Great Flood (524) must have been kept here. The most impressive structure in Heaven was a wheel on which carved wooden angels rotated (505, 550). Cohen (liv) believes that it surrounded God and represented the neo-Platonic doctrine of the spheres emanating from the deity. A similar wheel is depicted in the illustration of the 1547 Valenciennes *Passion*.

God, wearing gloves and a purple robe bordered with sable (551–52), sat on a wooden throne (512) with an iron footstool before him (562). Perhaps appearing with God was the Holy Spirit, for whom a pair of gloves is mentioned; this item suggests the use of a human or at least a life-sized figure to represent the third person of the Trinity (Cohen, liv). A curtain, symbolically perpetuating the mystery and secrecy surrounding the divinity, could be drawn around God. This is the only station for which we definitely know that there was a curtain.

Following the stage directions in the director's copies, Cohen identifies sixty-seven various stations, like the desert where John the Baptist preaches, a pool for Tubal the paralytic, and the tomb of Lazarus (lxxxiv). In actuality there must have been at least ninety-eight stations, since a priest was paid for making ninety-eight signs "de grosse lettre des Lieux sur le Hourt" (in big letters for the stations on stage [Cohen, 536]). Obviously, ninety-eight distinct locales could not have existed on the stage simultaneously. One location must have served for different scenes as long as it was labeled with the appropriate placard (Cohen, lxxxvii). For example, the pool for the paralytic could also have represented the Jordan River and the Sea of Galilee. Lazarus' tomb may have doubled as Christ's tomb. When Judas knocked down branches from his father's apple tree (an episode taken from Jean Michel), he may have done so from the same one that represented the tree of the forbidden fruit. Practical considerations for maximizing the use of space thus gave rise to typological associations that could be vividly and easily grasped since they were presented in such a direct and palpable manner.

In turn, typological associations could determine staging. For example, the stage direction "le logis de Marie et de Jhesus à XXX ans se fera, se on voeult, au logis de Adam" (if desired, the lodging of Mary and the 30-year old Jesus can be the same as Adam's [Cohen, 133]) calls for one *locus* to be used twice. Once a certain space is associated with a particular person, anyone using this space is seen as taking over the role of the original occupant. In the English mystery cycles, the devil, when usurping divine power, sits in God's throne. Christ and Mary, as the new Adam and Eve, herald a new existence, but one within the same world as that inhabited by the first man and woman. Having the two pairs share the same space is a highly visible manner of setting off the second as a fulfillment of the first. The staging and the text itself contract the world's history into a series of repeated events which, however, are sometimes recapitulated with significant variations.

The staging of the Mons *Passion*, though making use of figural props like the wheel of angels, aims toward realistic representation. The fruit trees, live animals, and fake blood (552) are used to make the action look as if it is actually happening. Realism here does not mean historical accuracy, but rather refers to the immediacy of the event and setting. Even though God and the devils have appropriate non-human characteristics like the ability to disappear, they are surrounded by earthly paraphernalia. God, in the costume of a king, sits on a throne, while the devils live in a fortress-like structure. The ineffable is materialized. God and Lucifer also act as humans do, and respectively rule like a benevolent king and a paranoid dictator.

THE STAGING OF CHRIST'S TRIALS AND CRUCIFIXION IN THE MONS *PASSION*[15]

Props and Costumes

knife
noose
tree
various chairs and thrones
old garment bordered with marten and ripped at the edges
white robe of a fool

---

[15] Although the script combines the texts of Gréban and Michel, this section of the Mons performance provides a close counterpart to the Third Day of Jodogne's edition and my translation. All the locations that appear here are also featured in Manuscript B of Gréban's *Passion*.

purple robe
robe without seams
bed (Procilla's)
basin and towel (used when Pilate washes his hands)
trumpet
crown of thorns
sticks
whips
four crosses (one hollow for Jesus to carry)
nails
cord
a die (for gambling for Jesus' seamless robe)
Veronica's cloth with Jesus' imprint
wine
drinking cup
tablet with inscription
lance
sponge
four ladders
hammers
pliers
flasks
boxes
ointment
stone
seals (for closing up the tomb)

Stations (listed in order of action)

1. Annas' tribunal
2. Caiaphas' tribunal
3. Hell
4. Judas' tree (for hanging)
5. Pilate's court
6. Herod's court
7. prison (where Barrabas and two thieves are kept)
8. Procilla's (Pilate's wife) apartment
9. carpenter
10. Mount Calvary
11. prison on Mount Calvary (where the two thieves are held before being crucified)
12. Nicodemus' place
13. Joseph of Arimathea's place
14. Jesus' tomb

15. Mary, St. John, and the three Marys either return to one station or to separate ones that are probably near one another.

The two most important settings, where much of the action takes place on the Third Day, are Pilate's court and Mount Calvary. Pilate's tribunal is square and contains two seats. One is tall and well-decorated, probably a throne; the other is not as tall. The stage directions for the *Mons Passion* are very explicit about when Pilate should sit in each. The taller one is reserved for official pronouncements, like the final condemnation of Christ (307) and delivering up Barrabas (326); the smaller one is for the interrogation of Christ. Usually only the two men remain inside the tribunal, and Christ is always led in or out of it, symbolizing his complete passivity during the trial. When Pilate announces his decisions to the Jews, he steps out from the tribunal, for they cannot enter it, since as a Pharisee explains, Passover tradition forbids it.

The Crucifixion must have been quite complicated, for it required an extra rehearsal (Cohen, 530).[16] The actor playing Christ was tied to the cross while it was on the ground. The cross was then raised, to be jarred into a kind of mortise that held it upright. The cross had two small supports on which the actor rested his arms (561). His hands were tied to the crossbeams. Since such a heavy cross would have been difficult to drag around the stage, the actor in the previous scene carried a hollow one (lxii).

SUMMARY

The following brief summary of the First, Second, and Fourth Days of Arnoul Gréban's *Mystère de la Passion* provides a framework for the Third Day, which is translated in its entirety. I have outlined many scenes in broad strokes, omitting specific arguments and most of the prologues since these usually consist of mere summary. I have also simplified the plot's movement by not indicating the frequent practice of intertwining scenes.

The first 1,510 lines, occurring before the First Day proper, recount the creation of the universe, the fall of Adam and Eve, Cain's murder of Abel, and Seth's failed attempt to obtain the oil of mercy for Adam and Eve.

The First Day begins with Adam, Eve, and the prophets wondering when redemption will come. There follows a 1,320-line debate

---

[16] We know that there were at least forty-eight rehearsals before the performance.

among Wisdom and the Four Daughters of God (Mercy, Justice, Truth, and Peace) on whether or not mankind should be redeemed. God resolves to send Christ, whereupon the play dramatizes in turn the Annunciation, the Visitation, Joseph's Doubt, the Nativity, the Shepherds' Visit, the Circumcision of Christ, the Gift of the Magi, the Presentation of Christ in the Temple, Herod's Wrath, the Flight into Egypt, the Slaughter of the Innocents, the Death of Herod, the Return to Nazareth, and Christ among the Doctors. The last episode includes a 733-line debate on the Incarnation among the doctors with the young Jesus occasionally participating. Interestingly, two of the Pharisees, Zorobabel, who argues that Christ is born, and Gamaliel, who argues the contrary, are the same two who reconfirm for Herod the news of Christ's birth after the Magi have left his court. In a previous scene, Gréban ironically has Herod consulting Annas and Caiaphas on the truth of the prophecies about Christ.

Also included in the First Day are four scenes involving devils: Lucifer worries about the liberation of the souls from Hell; Satan thinks Christ might be the Messiah; Satan proposes the Slaughter of the Innocents; the devils bring Herod's soul to Hell.

After a prologue, the Second Day opens with John the Baptist preaching repentance. This is followed by the temptation of Christ and the imprisonment of John the Baptist. Christ chooses his apostles while Judas Iscariot explains that he is wretched because he killed his father and married his mother. Christ, along with Mary and all the apostles, attends the wedding at Cana. Afterwards, Christ and the apostles leave for Judea where Christ literally blows away the money changers in the temple. Nicodemus visits Christ, who speaks to him about baptism and grace. During the course of his travels, Christ meets the Samaritan woman at the well and performs four healing miracles, reviving two dead women, exorcising a devil named Fergalus who then complains to Lucifer, and restoring a paralytic. Meanwhile Herod has John the Baptist beheaded. After performing his early miracles, Christ delivers and explains the parable of the sower and performs the miracle of the loaves and the fishes. The Transfiguration occurs, and Judas envies the three apostles who witness it. Christ publicly denounces the Pharisees, who retaliate by bringing forth the adulteress for judgment. While Christ dines at the house of Simon the Pharisee, Mary Magdalene anoints his feet. He heals a blind man and resuscitates Lazarus who later describes Hell. In a tender scene between mother and son, Mary expresses her fear of Christ's impending death while he explains that he must die. Meanwhile, several Jews who followed Christ and the Pharisees argue about the possibility of Christ's divinity. Annas advises that even if Christ is the Messiah, they would be foolish to support such a weak king. This discussion is especially significant because

Annas does not completely deny Christ as the Messiah but simply favors practical concerns. Caiaphas sends six soldiers to arrest Christ, but they do not find him because he is dining at the house of Simon the Leper. When the soldiers return empty-handed, Annas tells them to kill Lazarus. Christ enters Jerusalem and then returns to Bethany. In a famous scene adapted from the *Passion Isabeau*, Mary pleads with her son to remain, but he returns to Jerusalem and preaches against the Pharisees at the Temple. He then returns to Bethany. Meanwhile Satan tempts Judas into betraying Christ. Christ leaves Mary and goes to the Last Supper. On the Mount of Olives, Christ asks his Father if he must die, and God in turn asks Justice, who remains firm in her demand for Christ's death. The soldiers arrest Christ and Annas interrogates him. The soldiers mock and torture him, thus bringing the Second Day to a close. The text of the Third Day is translated below.

The Fourth Day begins where the Third ended, with the soldiers guarding the tomb of Christ. Caiaphas has Joseph of Arimathea arrested and imprisoned for having buried Christ. The three Marys buy ointment for Christ's body and the apostles lament his death. Lucifer, angry at having lost so many souls during the Harrowing of Hell, orders Satan to find out what happened to Christ. God decides to resurrect his son and sends angels to the tomb and to the three Marys. While the soldiers sleep, Christ appears to Mary, a rather unusual scene because typically Mary Magdalene is the first witness of the resurrection. The three Marys find the empty tomb, and the angels tell them of the resurrection. The guards awaken and, upon realizing that the body is missing, plan to protect themselves by explaining that Christ has risen. Mary Magdalene accompanies John and Peter to the tomb. In an apparent inconsistency, she now wonders who took the body away. Christ appears before her as a gardener and then appears to the two Marys and Peter. He appears to James and then delivers Joseph of Arimathea from jail. The jailkeepers tell Caiaphas of Joseph's disappearance, and the soldiers tell him of Christ's resurrection. Although they are not believed, they are bribed to keep silent. The soldiers then tell a worried Pilate that the body was stolen. He realizes that they fell asleep and is furious. Christ appears to the pilgrims at Emmaus and to the apostles including doubting Thomas. The Virgin rejoices with the three Marys and later tells them that she will be present at Christ's ascension. The apostles have a miraculous fishing catch. Satan reports the resurrection to Lucifer. The Virgin, the three Marys, the apostles, and Christ dine together, and then all witness his ascension. Christ greets God and the angels rejoice. The devils are furious that Christ is beyond their reach. Christ asks God to send down the Holy Spirit, who then descends upon the apostles, other followers, the holy women, and the Virgin. The final scene returns us to the beginning of the First Day in the court of heaven. The Four Daughters of God are fully at peace with one another. The final prologue offers a summary and asks the audience to be faithful.

TRANSLATOR'S PREFACE

Arnoul Gréban's *The Mystery of the Passion* presents two major difficulties for the translator. The first, common to any work of verse, is the problem of rendering the poetic diction of the original into modern English. Gréban's syntax can be especially complicated, but I have tried to retain it except in cases where the translation would sound too awkward. I have sought to achieve a balance between the pleasing strangeness of poetic language and the requirements of clarity. The second difficulty lies in Gréban's use of slang, which is largely confined to the tyrants and torturers. Some meanings are not recoverable, so the immediate context and later French slang have been my guides. I have avoided the modern practice of capitalizing pronouns referring to the divinity, thus following the original manuscript and eliminating the awkward problem of having evil characters refer to God with the respect that a capital letter confers. The line numbers correspond to Jodogne's edition, and stage directions from the Mons *Passion* are indicated by brackets.

The Mystery of the Passion
The Third Day

CHARACTERS IN ORDER OF APPEARANCE
IN THE THIRD DAY

Annas, former chief priest
Roillart, first soldier of Annas
Dentart, second soldier
Gadifer, third soldier
Dragon, servant of Annas
Gueulu, servant of Annas
Malchus, servant of Annas
Bruyant, second soldier of Caiaphas
Estonné, third soldier
Malcuidant, a soldier of Caiaphas
Celsidon, a merchant in the temple
Judas
Caiaphas, current chief priest
Jeroboam, First Pharisee
Mardocee, Second Pharisee
Naason, Third Pharisee
Elyachin, Fourth Pharisee
Bannanias, Fifth Pharisee
Joathan, Sixth Pharisee
Nachor, Sadducee
Nathan, Pharisee
Maucourant, messenger of Caiaphas
Emilius, bird seller
Rabanus, moneychanger
Nenbroth, a Jew

Salmanasar, cousin to Malchus
Phares, a Jew
Ruben, a Jew
Gedeon, a Jew
Neptalin, a Jew
Moab, a Jew
Abiron, a Jew
Tubal, a Jew
Celius, a Jew
Abacut, a Jew
Joram, Second Scribe
Isacar, Third Scribe
Jesus
Jacob, Scribe
Our Lady
Gabriel
Mary Magdalene
Mary Jacobi
Mary Salome
Barraquin, Pilate's Usher
Pilate
Griffon, torturer belonging to Pilate's court
Claquedent, second torturer
Orillart, third torturer
Brayart, fourth torturer
Lucifer
Despair
Berich, devil
Astaroth, devil
Fergalus, devil
Cerberus, devil
Herod the Tetrarch
Radigon, count in Herod's court
Amphirarus, knight in Herod's court
Groignart, servant in Herod's court
Brutaumont, jailkeeper of Pilate
Barrabas
Broyefort, Pilate's page
Adam
Eve
God
Michael, archangel
Isaiah
Ezekiel

Jeremiah
David
Satan
Pilate's Wife
Sardina, her maid
Dymas, good thief
Gestas, bad thief
Carpenter
Blacksmith
Pilate's Trumpeter
Centurion
Rubion, first soldier of Centurion
Ascanius, second soldier of Centurion
Julia
Veronica
Perusina
Pasithea
Joseph of Arimathea
Simon of Cyrene
Saint John
Saint Denis of Athens
Empedocles
Raphael, archangel
Uriel, archangel
Jesus' Spirit
John the Baptist
Longinus
Nicodemus
Silk Merchant
Spice Merchant
Emilius, third soldier of Centurion

Prologue to the Third Day of the Passion of Our Lord Jesus Christ

To continue the subject matter
which is beneficial and perfect
to hearts full of compassion   19,908
and which treats in order
and in full, the high Passion
that brought forth our redemption
for our salvation—   19,912
before our beginning,
each one of us will hail
the Virgin in contemplation
and we will humbly say   19,916
with devotion, *Ave Maria.*

Ave Maria.

This devout salutation being finished,
lords, I humbly beg you to
lend a little silence   19,920
and ready your understanding
to take in the compassion,
charity, and perfect love
to which this passion leads   19,924
and joins all human nature.
Think that he who teaches himself
from this book, reaps great fruit
and that there is no story in this world   19,928
so fertile or so fecund
or which makes the heart
more attentive to the good to which it must tend.
He who listens to it well and understands it well,   19,932

desires to do no evil
but judges all earthly pleasure
wicked, deceiving, and momentary,
and there is no adversity so strong   19,936
that he does not bear patiently.
For when he thinks about
the fortune that comes his way,
he does not lose control,   19,940
but later, when he considers
that the blessed son of God
suffered and endured so much
to purify our filth,   19,944
he finds that what he endures
is nothing compared to the burden
that Jesus chose to carry for man.
Thus his wishes are moderated,   19,948
as he consults this mirror °
where every heart, to heal its affliction,
must profoundly observe itself.
And so that you may look at yourselves   19,952
and sweetly contemplate there,
we set before your eyes
this devout mirror for your benefit,
physically, through characters.   19,956
Observe yourselves and you will indeed be wise.
Each one glimpses his form there.
He who observes himself well, sees himself well.
May God grant that we observe so well,   19,960
that through looking, we behold,
after this mortal life,
the powerful immortal essence
which reigns without ever ceasing.   19,964
Lords, let us retrace a little
what was shown to you yesterday:
first was displayed before you
the celebrated and accomplished baptism   19,968
which St. John preached in the desert,
as minister and precursor
of Jesus Christ Our Lord.
Then you saw reference made to   19,972

19,949 The next several lines pun on the word *mirouer*, meaning "mirror" and
"exemplum," and *mirer*, "to look; to contemplate."

the feat of the forty days
during which Christ fasted
while the devil harshly assailed him.
Then you had a demonstration   19,976
of how, because of the reprimand
St. John gave to Herod,
he beheaded and killed him.
Then you saw Jesus gather   19,980
his disciples and assemble them together.
And then he changed water into wine
at the wedding of the host in Cana.
You saw him come to the temple   19,984
and banish the merchants outside,
for which they were roused against him.
And then, concerning Nicodemus,
how by night he set forth   19,988
to be a disciple of Jesus Christ.
And then the woman of Samaria
who came to draw from the well
and whom Christ converted through his preaching.   19,992
Then the high prince's daughter
and the widow's son
to whom, by his grace, he restored their souls.
Afterwards, the daughter of the Canaanite woman   19,996
was healed by Jesus.
After that there were words
on the transfiguration
when he shone forth like gold   20,000
on the mountain of Tabor.
Then you saw Mary Magdalene
who, full of the seven deadly sins,
obtained her pardon through good means   20,004
above Simon the Pharisee.
Afterwards, how the man born blind
was by him given light,
for which the Jews conceived great envy   20,008
and who murmured about it.
Then you beheld
the valiant lord Lazarus
whom Jesus raised from death   20,012
and with great power resuscitated him,
for which the Pharisees all the more insistently
sought to cause his death.
And after, for a brief while,   20,016

you beheld the unguent
with which Mary came to anoint him;
for which Judas sought to separate himself
from the love of the very gentle Jesus   20,020
because of the great anger it caused him.
After that you could see him mounted
on the ass in humility,
and he came to the renowned city   20,024
where there was great joy.
Then you saw various councils,
various false and wicked means
which the perverse Jews sought,   20,028
to know how they would take Jesus;
among them crept in
Judas who made a deal with them,
that for the price of thirty *deniers* °   20,032
he would readily give him to them.
After this, the supper was given
during which he again revealed to his disciples
his great and perfect humility   20,036
when he washed all their feet.
Precisely there he established
the holy and divine sacrament,
beneficial to all the disciples   20,040
except Judas who was unclean,
and whom you soon saw leave
to carry out his betrayal.
And then in a pleasant place   20,044
called the Garden of Olivet
you saw Jesus humbled
and supplicate God, his father,
because of the fear and terrible dread   20,048
lodged in his heart.
There the angel appeared
and gently comforted him.
After you saw Judas instruct   20,052
his henchmen and guide them
in forcefully seizing
Jesus, our blessed Savior,
and as soon as they approached,   20,056

20,032 *denier*, a monetary unit. One *livre* equals 20 *sous*; one *sou* equals twelve
deniers (Cohen, lxxviii)

you saw how they stumbled.
And then concerning saint Peter
who cut the servant's ear.
Then you could see him being brought   20,060
and pitifully conducted
by Satan's ministers
into the house of Annas
where St. Peter had such weak faith   20,064
that he denied him three times.
Then you saw Annas go to bed
and command his servants
to guard him, which they did,   20,068
and they hurled great abuse at him.
Thus we labored so,
till we stopped at this point.
Now we wish to continue   20,072
with Jesus, how they deliver him
to Caiaphas to distress,
probe, and examine him.
There you will see inquiries,   20,078
false witnesses, accusations,
and all the tricks one may try
to cause an innocent to die.
Afterwards we will show you   20,080
the severe despair
to which Judas gave himself
when he saw his master condemned.
You will also see Pilate   20,084
who took great pains
to find the tricks and the means
to appease the citizens
and who labored with great effort   20,088
to secure Jesus Christ's escape.
And to shorten this prologue
and come to the event without delaying,
we intend   20,092
to pursue this glorious mystery
until the moment
when the body will have been removed from
the cross, by his good friends,   20,096
to be put into his sepulchre.
And placing him in the sepulchre,
we will then rest.
We therefore humbly beg you   20,100

that before our beginning
you will give us silence,
and soon you will see us ready.

ANNAS Now has Phoebus traveled so far   20,104
with Phaeton and led
his exceedingly swift horses
that in his natural course,
he has quickly encompassed   20,108
and circled all the earth
till with his glowing face
he has so richly colored
this mild and pleasant morning   20,112
that it seems golden.
The very gracious Vespra °
and Aurora have appeared;
they have made known the news   20,116
of the very mild morning
in which all joyous hearts delight.
And it seems to me that this night
has lasted like forty   20,120
because of the great and burning desire
I have to achieve something
I feel enclosed in my heart;
whether sleeping or dozing   20,124
I can never forget it.
And the matter so affects me
that I have not slept
this night except fitfully;   20,128
and today nothing would please me
so much as my plan's
being executed
and entirely realized.   20,132
ROILLART When I look at this false scoundrel
who has sown so much discord
and done so much filthy work,
my teeth grind in hatred.   20,136
DENTART ° Will he definitely obtain pardon,

20,114 *Vesperuz.* Latin name for the planet Venus as it appears at sunset (Jodogne, 362).
20,137 Several of the torturers' names are meaningful.
    Claquedent—"chattering teeth"

evil traitor that he is?

GADIFFER He'll get the bloody gibbet.
Our lords hold him too much in disfavor.   20,140

ROILLART He doesn't know that he's in a stew
for having corrupted the good people.

DENTART What?

ROILLART He's cooked his own goose. °
The heat's being turned on him!   20,144

DENTART I'll certainly burst with pain
if he doesn't get the bloody gibbet.

GADIFFER Roillart, before he gets away from us
let's hit him a little bit;   20,148
five or six lashes with a good whip
would be just right for him.
He has such a nice wide back
to receive a few good blows from a stick.   20,152

ROILLART Then let's begin; let's have some fun
by giving him some nice bruises.

DENTART Hey Roillart, you're getting excited.
You aren't waiting for your friends.   20,156

ROILLART I can't help it. Let's strike, let's strike
this false miserable seducer!
Take that, you knave!

DENTART Take that, false enchanter
and get your just desserts. °   20,160

ANNAS I wonder what my people are doing
on this pleasant morning.
They are worthless and lazy.
I expect that they are asleep.   20,164
No people were ever reprimanded
as much as they will be if this is so.
I would like to see what's going on
to be a little more sure.   20,168
Roillart!

ROILLART Your wish, my lord?

Dentart—"long-toothed"
Dragon—"standard"
Estonné—"frightened"
Malcuidant—"bad thinker"
Gueulu—"tricky" (*gueule, gorlé*)
20,143 *Il a fait ses pastés.* Literally, "He has made his pastries (or paté)." The torturers are distinguished by their use of food imagery.
20,160 *et taste quelz poires ce sont!* Literally, "and taste what pears these are!"

~ 11 ~

ANNAS Are you sleeping?

ROILLART No. We're awake.

ANNAS What are you doing?

DENTART We're rousing
    this official a tiny bit.   20,172
    Since his head hurts him,
    we're putting it back into shape a little.
    Isn't this good?

ANNAS It is so well said
    that one could not chatter better.   20,176
    Now then we must resolve
    his affair. We delay too long.
    Untie him from there right away
    and quickly bring him   20,180
    before me.

GADIFFER Now then come.
    Our lord, you must be untied
    but you'll be tied even higher
    before evening comes.   20,184

ROILLART Your filthy carcass has run
    into misfortune because of your sin. °

DENTART How well tied he is!
    There was no risk of his escaping.   20,188

GADIFFER Move. You must come
    talk to our chief.

ROILLART He's laughing.

DENTART True, but his teeth are barely showing.
    He laughs like last year's lamb.   20,192

ANNAS I see no other way
    to get a prompt judgment
    than to bring him quickly
    to the high priest, Caiaphas,   20,196
    who is the chief pontiff this year
    and who will examine him appropriately.

ROILLART Whoever would do him justice,
    would hang him on the spot.   20,200

ANNAS It is not for us to judge.
    As long as it concerns his misdeeds,
    his trial shall be carried out
    according to justice and equity   20,204

20,186 *En mal an.* A proverbial phrase (Hassell, 39). I have translated it as "misfortune."

and he will be punished justly
because he has trespassed and done wrong.
And so that everything be carried out °
according to the ways of reason,   20,208
soldiers, bring him to the house
of Caiaphas in this state.

DENTART There can be found also the entire assembly
of Pharisees, lords,   20,212
Scribes, and governors
who rule today.

ANNAS Greet the high priest for me
with honor and joy   20,216
and say that I send him
this wicked man through you
and that he should do with him all
that seems proper.   20,220

GADIFFER Don't you want us to recite to him
some of his past, fair deeds?

ANNAS No, no. He knows enough about them.
One need not declare them to him.   20,224
Besides, it won't be long before
I go to the assembly.

ROILLART May you be filled with joy
and honor for all your life.   20,228
Come on, come on. Make that wretch
walk forward; it's high time.

DENTART Walk. May the devil take him!
Are you walking slowly, like a bride?   20,232

MALCUIDANT Where is this crew going
now, so scattered about?

GADIFFER Our booty has been discovered.

DRAGON And where is this crew going?   20,236

ROILLART We are going to raise a little money
at Caiaphas' place.

GUEULU You never know what can happen,
but I wouldn't be so stupid
as to pay for work like that.   20,040

MALCUS And where is this crew going
now, so scattered about?

DENTART You're nothing but a beast in man's clothing.
Don't you see that we're bringing   20,244

20,207 *parfait*. A pun meaning "to be carried out" and "perfect."

this hypocrite that we've got
to present to our high leader?
BRUYANT This will not be without trouble,
since our lords don't like him one bit.   20,248
ESTONNÉ He will be punished.
GADIFFER Who doubts it?
Isn't he liable to receive punishment
for the mad presumption
with which he completely destroyed our law?   20,252
MALCUIDANT Let's go, friends, and join in.
Let's follow to see what will happen.
DRAGON He'll never escape from this;
the devil has guided him well.   20,256
CELSIDON He'll be escorted by us
to see what's to be done with him.
JUDAS Lords, look to your business.
Here is the one whom you hate so much   20,260
brought before you quite speedily,
accompanied by a great multitude and great noise.
I think that last night I delivered him
so very well into their hands that   20,264
he could not prevent his being
captured and bound.
Whether I have acted foolishly or well,
my conscience is bound up by it.   20,268
However, I call to your attention
that I have fulfilled my obligation to you.
CAIAPHAS You are released from your part of the bargain.
We can't ask anything more of you.   20,272
It is sufficient that we have him.
This business has been very well conducted.
JUDAS I am going, then.
JEROBOAM May God guide you!
You have acquitted yourself very well.   20,276
ROILLART Sir, may the great God of Israel
grant you to do his will.
Annas, my revered master,
and your faithful friend,   20,280
sends you this criminal
as a special present
since you are the high inquisitor
to whom such cases fall.   20,284
As he says,
you have been made fully aware of

what his deeds are and what they brought about.

CAIAPHAS He has not lied.

I know of his terrible crime,   20,288
much more than I should like to,
but then everyone murmurs about it.
Thus it is by necessity
that his deceit and his offense   20,292
should come to my attention.
Now, come here wretched man!
You were certainly born in an evil hour
to carry out the trickery and lead the life   20,296
of which everyone accuses you
though I do not believe
the bad reports in several respects;
the evil would be too great!   20,300
Now then, answer my question! °
Is it true that through your preaching
you want to destroy and oppose
the noble governance and the rule   20,304
with which the law guides and rules us?
Have you shown arrogance
against the law of Moses?
We are told that you and yours   20,308
reject and take no account of it
and make a new spiritual law
of which only you are able to speak.
Here you must make known to us   20,312

20,301–332 The parallel scene in the *Passion d'Arras* is changed by Gréban in several ways. First, Gréban's Christ is questioned about his teachings for the second time as Caiaphas closely repeats the questions posed by Annas in the Second Day (Combarieu du Grès and Subrenat, 511). In the *Passion d'Arras*, these questions are asked only once and only by Caiaphas towards the end of the Second Day (lines 12,234–61). Second, Christ responds to Annas with an answer from John 18:20–21, "I have spoken openly," etc., but in the Third Day he remains silent before Caiaphas. In the *Passion d'Arras*, Christ also answers Caiaphas, again citing John 18:20–21. Third, Gréban has Christ maintain silence during Caiaphas' probing until about 400 lines later when he answers the question, "Are you the true son of God?" (lines 20,720–27). In the *Passion d'Arras*, Caiaphas poses this question almost immediately after asking Christ about his teachings (lines 12,294–99). In summary, what appears as one brief unified scene in Marcadé becomes in Gréban's treatment two separate and much longer scenes, bridging two days. The latter, confining Christ's dialogue to speeches from the gospels and the apocryphal *Gospel of Nicodemus*, has him remain silent for much longer periods of time, thus emphasizing his humility, patience, and suffering. He is a much more dignified Christ.

from where comes this law which you proclaim,
whether God revealed it to you
or if you devised it?
If you tell us it comes from you,   20,316
it is not right for us to uphold it
since you are not of authority
to shape it according to your will.
If you tell us God made it,   20,320
then you consider yourself a great prophet
because God approaches you so closely
that he reveals his secrets to you
and you consider yourself, as you argue,   20,324
as holy as or holier than Moses,
to the extent that you want to reform
that which Moses wanted to form.
Now prepare yourself to answer   20,328
and to reveal the plan
of your action as you understand it.

Pause

Answer! What are you waiting for?
Do you hear my question?   20,332
JEROBOAM He has no desire
to give you any answer.
MARDOCEE Yes he has, but he fears misfortune.
He is thinking over what he'll answer.   20,336
NAASON He will conduct himself very cleverly,
so that if he answers you, he won't make a mistake,
for, whatever side he takes,
he'll run into trouble.   20,340
CAIAPHAS Will you not otherwise speak?
You are before the tribunal.
Is it true that you have committed
the acts of which you are accused?   20,344
It is said that you have fooled
the public with a false teaching
and that you know the art of magic,
using it whenever you please.   20,348
Answer!
ELYACHIN He has no words.
You should provoke him.
CAIAPHAS Lords, what's this? Look
how this scoundrel behaves!   20,352
It seems he does not pay attention to

anything I ask him.
He will perish because he does not deign
to answer a word to my question,   20,356
and yet I am quite certain that he hears me
posing my questions loudly and clearly.
BANNANIAS A procedure other than this one is needed,
since you see that on this point   20,360
he does not speak or answer at all;
Maybe this is a trick,
so that he says no word
prejudicial to him.   20,364
CAIAPHAS Bannanias, worthy man,
please tell us what better
and more expedient means there are
of presenting our case.   20,368
BANNANIAS Since it pleases you that I explain it,
dear sir, the matter is as follows:
since he devotes himself
to concealing his offenses,   20,372
we should resolve
to know them by another means
and to look everywhere for witnesses
who have some knowledge of his actions.   20,376
This way we can increase
his troubles and accuse him,
for when it comes to the proof,
there must be many   20,380
who will be witnesses to the errors
in which he has long lived.
And so if he is convicted
of any allegation that mandates death,   20,384
it will not be necessary to inquire further.
We have our sentence.
CAIAPHAS Your judgment
stems from a very perceptive intellect.   20,388
Joathan, what do you think?
I would like to hear you again.
JOATHAN He speaks well.
CAIAPHAS And you, Nachor,
tell us your thoughts.   20,392
NACHOR The plan is so well thought out
that you will never have a better scheme.
NATHAN Here then is what you will do.
Summon me your herald   20,396

and order him immediately
to announce loudly and clearly
that, if someone can speak
on Jesus' deeds, for or against, 20,400
he should appear before you and present himself
to give his report
on pain of having his goods
seized and of having his body 20,404
subjected to great pain.
CAIAPHAS It is well spoken, and I agree.
It shall be done without fail.
Maucourant!
MAUCOURANT Wha'!
CAIAPHAS What an idiot!
Hear his manner, 20,408
responding "wha'" to the lords.
He is full of good and honor!
MAUCOURANT Who's there?
JACOB My lord
calls you. Did you hear him? 20,412
MAUCOURANT Who doubts it? So help me, yes.
But I didn't know who it was.
My dear lord, may God give you joy!
Do you wish to command me to do something? 20,416
CAIAPHAS Yes, but it seems to me that one must
send for you like a lord.
Now go quickly proclaim
throughout this noble and good city 20,420
that if there is today some person
to whom this Jesus has done wrong,
he should come to oppose with all his force
his being set free. 20,424
And if a man should come forward
to complain about his malice,
he shall be treated with such fairness and justice
that he will be happy. 20,428
MAUCOURANT Sir, my will strives
only to fulfill your wish.
I am going to deliver your message
exactly as you have framed it. 20,432
Hear ye, hear ye, hear ye
all citizens and inhabitants,
even if there were ten times as many
in this renowned city! 20,436

At the request of Caiaphas,
a matter is set forth through me,
which can greatly affect you.
Know that our lords now have,   20,440
at their assembly, Jesus,
who has been arrested and seized
because he did harm
and injustice to many people.   20,444
If there is a man whom he injures
or has injured in the past,
he should come forth to accuse him,
and he will be closely listened to.   20,448
EMILIUS He's as good as dead, it seems to me,
even if there were ten thousand like him.
RABANUS This is done to ensure a fair trial,
to hear the opponents   20,452
and those who will hurt him.
If I can, I'll not fail to respond.
NENBROTH I'll quickly follow you.
Soon we'll work well.   20,456
RABANUS How's that?
NENBROTH We'll earn our share
if you get my drift. °
EMILIUS How?
NENBROTH Here's the way.
Our lords, as you know,   20,460
feel greatly vexed
by this Jesus who is too caustic toward them °
and, in short, they hate him to death.
So, if we wish to work well   20,464
we only need to testify
against him, from whence he emerges,
whether good or bad, true or false
or completely obvious lying.   20,468
Provided that it results in Jesus' perishing,
we shall gain their favor without fail
and if the falsehood succeeds,
we will receive some reward on the side.   20,472
SALMANASAR That's not stupidly said.

20,458 *se vous enssuyvez ma chançon*. Literally, "if you follow my song."
20,462–63 Both lines end with the word *mort*. The first is a verb meaning "to be
mordant" and the second is the noun meaning "death."

It's well thought out in legal style.

PHARÉS Come on. This is the moment for those wanting to do
    something to get to it.
    Let's go.   20,476

RUBEN Gideon, my very dear friend,
    I have learned bad news.
    We are told that Jesus has been seized
    and put into the hands of the lords.   20,480

GIDEON They are evil executioners.
    If they can, they will destroy him.

NEPTALIN Let's find out what they will do with him.
    They are crafty and malicious.   20,484

MOAB Alas, what wrong has he done them
    that they feel such strong hatred for him?

ABIRON This is all because of the good teaching
    which he introduced to the people.   20,488

TUBAL Let's go. Everyone is running there.
    This is a good sign that it's true.

CELIUS I'm going there.

ABACUT I'll follow you,
    for I greatly desire to see him.   20,492

CAIAPHAS Now my lords, since I see you all together,
    I would like to tell you
    the reason I have gathered you together
    according to the advice of the governors,   20,496
    many of whom are here.
    It is evident and certain
    that we have been presented
    with this man of evil repute   20,500
    called Jesus by his proper name,
    as many men are certain.
    He is charged with numerous serious crimes
    to be discussed according to the laws.   20,504
    Notwithstanding this, however,
    we want to inquire among you
    if there is anyone from some land
    who can speak of his offenses,   20,508
    of five or six of the most serious,
    for I think there are too many
    to say them all at once.
    It would not be done in haste.   20,512

NENBROTH My lords, I tell you he
    overturns the law and destroys it
    by his fraud and his deceit.

He gathers a great assembly   20,516
of common people from Galilee,
who ignore the law,
to follow him.
SALMANASAR What he tells you
is true, as I assure you,   20,520
and in fact, I swear to you
that I was in the area and the place
where he openly said
to the people gathered there   20,524
that he was begotten in the world
before Abraham was born.
Know where his reason finds its support,
for it is not intelligible.   20,528
CAIAPHAS Here is something truly impossible
and the most insane thing ever,
if it is true.
SALMANASAR I attest to it.
Many people heard him,   20,532
some of whom responded by saying
that he had Beelzebub in his body.
CAIAPHAS I believe that these are great transgressions
against reason and against God.   20,536
PHARÉS And I was in another place,
not in one only but in five or six,
where he healed and cured
the sick with I don't know what kind of power,   20,540
and he used the art of medicine,
transgressing our Sabbath.
And when asked by the people passing there
why he was doing this,   20,544
he answered that it was within his power
and that God in the heavenly realm
labored very well that day, °
by which fact he could work then as well.   20,548
CAIAPHAS Also, we must consider that
he wants to put himself forth
as the son of the living God
since he has similar power.   20,552
JEROBOAM He offers enough demonstration
to back up such boasting.

20,547 John 5:17

~ 21 ~

RABANUS It is wholly his mark and design.
　　　　He has said in more than ten places,　　　　　　　　20,556
　　　　that he descended from the high heavens,
　　　　and in order to be better-known,
　　　　says that his father and he are one.
　　　　He also usurps and attributes　　　　　　　　　　20,560
　　　　to himself divine power,
　　　　a highly unorthodox proposition
　　　　from which will come a great evil
　　　　if no remedy is found.　　　　　　　　　　　　　20,564
CAIAPHAS Here is something poorly controlled,
　　　　lords, and a distressing account.
　　　　A man who had no favor
　　　　would experience the ordeal of death,　　　　　　20,568
　　　　assuming that one proves him guilty,
　　　　by witnesses, of all these cases here.
　　　　What do you think of this?
　　　　I beg you to think　　　　　　　　　　　　　　20,572
　　　　if there are not enough grounds
　　　　for executing him.
JEROBOAM Sir, subject to correction from
　　　　you and my lords present,　　　　　　　　　　　20,576
　　　　I will tell you what I think about it.
　　　　It is my opinion that all these imputations,
　　　　which have been set forth in many articles,
　　　　lack sufficient weight　　　　　　　　　　　　　20,580
　　　　for this wicked person
　　　　to be sentenced to death according to the law.
MARDOCEE It seems so to me.
　　　　Even though he has thus transgressed,　　　　　20,584
　　　　for which reason he has been attacked,
　　　　he confesses nothing,
　　　　and our law requires and rules
　　　　that the sinner avow his wrong　　　　　　　　　20,588
　　　　and confess before he perishes;
　　　　Jesus does not hurry towards this.
　　　　On the other hand, let us put forth the case
　　　　in which he spoke of Eve or Adam　　　　　　　20,592
　　　　or of Noah or Abraham,
　　　　that he said he was born before them;
　　　　these are the words of a madman
　　　　or of a booby or a lunatic;　　　　　　　　　　20,596
　　　　they require that he be well beaten
　　　　without pity or mercy

so that he no longer have any appetite for them.
But to condemn him to death,   20,600
I would not dare dream of it.
On the other hand, if it is said that he enjoys
breaking our Sabbath,
he must incur some punishment   20,604
but not death.
Therefore, he who wishes his death,
must seek another path,
one that is a little more subtle.   20,608

CAIAPHAS Wretched man, why don't you answer?
Are you so deaf, dumb, or blind,
that you behave like an ass,
not defending your case?   20,612
Do you not hear at all the terrible crimes
which these people report about you?
Do you not hear how they attack you?
What is wrong with you that you do not answer them   20,616
or that you do not give them a single answer
if you feel that you are somehow right?

NAASON He will never speak openly.
Look at him lower his face   20,620
towards the ground.

ELYACHIN It is his manner;
do not pay such close attention.

NENBROTH I assure you that he obstructs
and strongly opposes   20,624
the rights of Caesar the emperor
and does not cease plotting
to draw the people to him,
so that the crown is usurped   20,628
and he is made king of Judea,
which must rouse you, my lords,
as guardians and protectors
of the high imperial rights.   20,632

CAIAPHAS Have you perpetrated such crimes,
evil and infamous seducer?
Do you pretend to our kingdom?
What right to it can you claim?   20,636
And are you a man who can govern,
you who are full of misery?

EMILIUS My lords, before we consider
his case, please hear us,   20,640
for we want publicly

to prove him guilty of criminal charges.
CAIAPHAS Go ahead then, make your preamble,
    so that we may act quickly.   20,644
EMILIUS Sir, my companion and I °
    swear to you, as true,
    that before several men of the law
    he made it known and said,   20,648
    "I certainly have the power to destroy
    this temple and to demolish it completely
    and then, to rebuild it
    in only three days."   20,652
CAIAPHAS Here are very well rehearsed lies
    and quite obvious bragging;
    for no one, no matter how foolhardy,
    could put together in three whole days   20,656
    such a work on which more than a thousand workers
    worked for forty years.
    Doesn't this seem reason enough
    for subjecting him to a painful death?   20,660
JACOB It is nothing but a vain speech,
    dear sir, and, to speak frankly,
    one must not dwell on it;
    and to put him to death for that reason,   20,664
    I am not in agreement.
    The law cannot bring him forth to execution.
    Moreover, this would have the effect of provoking
    the people, to our great shame.   20,668
JORAM It would cause us too great a scandal
    to kill him for so little,
    and as my master has said here,
    the reason is somewhat too meager.   20,672
    But to prick him a little more keenly,
    it is worthwhile that we inquire
    if he is either a murderer or a thief,
    a spy or a highwayman.   20,676
    These means of destroying him are more
    in keeping with our honor.
ISACAR There will not be much to do,
    seeing that he roams the countryside   20,680
    with a great crowd of scoundrels
    who live without laboring.

20,645 Matthew 26:60–61; Mark 14:57–58.

Since they know only how to feast
and die of hunger and cold,   20,684
they will soon be
forced to commit a crime.
CAIAPHAS I am dying of grief and distress
over this case which affects me greatly.   20,688
I'm gnashing my teeth, °
and my heart's swelling with hatred.
If this man must obtain reprieve,
my days will finish in pain.   20,692
Come here, man full of misery, °
why don't you respond to the
cutting and stinging incriminations
against your reputation and fame?   20,696
Do you not fear shame or slander?
You hear that your honor is wounded
and by your idiocy or stupidity
you jeopardize yourself.   20,700

Pause

JEROBOAM You are lecturing in vain,
he will never do anything else.
CAIAPHAS Come now. Is there a man who will accuse
him of committing   20,704
known larceny
or murdering or robbing anyone,
either him or his people, it's all the same?
If anyone has any information,   20,708
he should reveal it publicly.
It is all that we ask.
MARDOCEE My lord, we are making a mistake.
Not a soul responds to this question.   20,712
CAIAPHAS Because I cannot condemn this man,
such tremendous anger pierces my heart
that I think one should smother
my heart, since it oppresses me heavily.   20,716
But I have thought of another trick
with which I shall be able to confound him,
and force him to answer.

20,689 *les dens me serrent en la bouche.* Literally, "my teeth are grinding in my mouth."
20,693 Matthew 26:62–63; Mark 14:60–61.

Now, come here, evil creature. °   20,720
Approach me. I adjure you,
by the living God who created
heaven and earth and all that is,
to tell us in this place   20,724
if you are Christ, the son of God,
about whom the prophets have written.
Now answer me that.
JESUS It is you who have said it.
But in truth, I say to you also   20,728
that henceforth you will see
the son of man in brilliant glory
seated at the right hand of God the father
and coming from the eternal realm   20,732
within the clouds of the sky
in power and great force.
CAIAPHAS Here is the most outrageous blasphemy
that I have ever heard in my life!   20,736
He blasphemes with his speech.
What need is there to go further
to find witnesses against him?

Here Caiaphas tears his clothing and says again

You yourselves hear his blasphemy.   20,740
What do you think?
JEROBOAM Take him away. Take him away.
He deserves a painful death.
You hear how he places himself
above the law in every way.   20,744
CAIAPHAS Will such errors be tolerated
by which this scoundrel dishonors our laws?
What do you think?
MARDOCEE Take him away. Take him away.
He deserves a painful death.   20,748
CAIAPHAS If you do not find a solution
and his great wickedness is realized,
you will shortly see us
lost, exiled, and ruined.   20,752
What do you think?
NAASON Take him away. Take him away.

20,720–40 Matthew 26:63–66; Mark 14:62–64; Luke 22:62–71; *Passion d'Arras* (lines 12,294–311).

He deserves a painful death.
You hear how he places himself
above the law in every way.   20,756
CAIAPHAS And so, you then consent
to his death to speed up the case?
It only remains for him to be judged
by the criminal procurator.   20,760
Do I speak rightly?
ELYACHIM Quite rightly indeed.
We are all of the opinion
that he deserves death
without your further examining him.   20,764
CAIAPHAS Bannanias, decide,
do you think his death would be good?
BANNANIAS I give him the death sentence
and consent to it fully.   20,768
CAIAPHAS And you, Joathan?
JOATHAN Likewise
I certainly approve of his death.
CAIAPHAS And you there, Nachor?
NACHOR I agree with him.
CAIAPHAS Jacob?   20,772
JACOB We must put an end to him.
CAIAPHAS Nathan?
NATHAN His death is necessary
and quite advantageous to all of us.
CAIAPHAS Isacar?
ISACAR Why do you ask?
Each one of us agrees   20,776
that if he could suffer a hundred deaths,
we should make him do so.
CAIAPHAS It is no longer necessary to hold council
to conduct this affair;   20,780
you are all content that he die
without disagreeing on anything.
ALL TOGETHER *Fiat*, we are all in agreement °
and are all in league with one another.   20,784
CAIAPHAS We must no longer seek disputes,
we are in agreement on this point.
Lords, put yourselves at ease.

20,783 *Fyat*, "so be it." An expression traditionally used to express submission to
God (Combarieu di Grès and Subrenat, 513).

Dragon, Bruyant, and Estonné! 20,788
BRUYANT Is this villain left
    to our good command?
CAIAPHAS Yes, do to him
    the bloody worst that you can. 20,792
    You cannot harm him enough
    to content us.
BRUYANT That suffices. Since we hear you,
    we will obey your word. 20,796
MALCUIDANT God, he has received a windfall in
    being paid such wages.
MALCUS Dare you sow such lies,
    wretch who has become even more wretched? 20,800
DRAGON In front of our high and wise lords,
    do you dare sow such lies?
GUEULU You preach to the people and speak
    wholly against the law. 20,804
ESTONNÉ Say, wretch,
    do you dare sow such lies,
    wretch who has become even more wretched?

They spit in his face

BRUYANT Fie on the rogue fallen into roguery!
ALCUIDANT Fie on the false, traitorous enchanter! 20,808
BRUYANT It's too bad that he wasn't burned
    ten years ago, this false deceiver.
DRAGON Fie on the thief!
GUEULU Fie on the liar!
ESTONNÉ Fie on the disloyal rascal! 20,812
BRUYANT Fie on the most evil deceiver
    under the heavens.
CAIAPHAS Go forth bravely, comrades.
    Dress him as you can. 20,816
MALCUIDANT We're attacking him violently.
JEROBOAM Go forth bravely, comrades.
    Deal him pain and torment
    without flinching; you have permission. 20,820
MALCUS He has received so many blows,
    that I think his eyes have burst.
CAIAPHAS Go forth bravely, comrades.
    Dress him as you can. 20,824
    If I see you hesitating,
    thieves, I'll have you arrested.
BRUYANT And then, after that, what?

CAIAPHAS Hung
    on a gibbet, feet up, head down.   20,828
BRUYANT Then we won't hesitate,
    if it depends only on that.
    Estonné, grab him there,
    let's place him at the bottom here,   20,832
    and then we will amuse ourselves
    by beating him over the head.
ESTONNÉ Come on, false, dishonest sorcerer,
    be humble.   20,836
MALCUIDANT Fie!
ESTONNÉ What's the matter with you?
MALCUIDANT He is so smeared
    with spit from top to bottom
    that it turns my stomach
    to look at him in the face.   20,840
DRAGON That was badly spoken, saving your grace.
    That word is far too good for him.
MALCUIDANT To look at him in the muzzle: °
    do you want me to call it that?   20,844
DRAGON That's better.
GUEULU Bah, forget that.
    You're sustaining a meager argument.
    Tomorrow is Sabbath day.
    Hey comrades, let's take care of our business.   20,848
MALCUS For this, he must be shaken up
    a little more furiously.
BRUYANT First, I would like to know
    how they want us to hit him.   20,852
JEROBOAM With our fists.
BRUYANT Rather with very big sticks.
    That way we won't hurt ourselves as much.
ESTONNÉ Now let's strike him in different ways.
MALCUIDANT With our fists.   20,856
ESTONNÉ Rather with very big sticks.
DRAGON Hey comrades, we're wasting time.
    Let's batter him without yakking.
GUEULU With our fists.
DRAGON Rather with very big sticks.

20,843 Malcuidant, at Dragon's reminder, corrects himself and substitutes the word "muzzle" to refer to Christ's face. The tyrants often use words specifically reserved for animals to refer to Christ's body.

That way we won't hurt ourselves as much. 20,860
GUEULU All in play and fun,
    I'll give him a whale of a blow. °
MALCUS And as a dirty fighter,
    I'll give him one too. 20,864
BRUYANT By God, since everyone treats him
    so harshly, I must do it too.
ESTONNÉ What do you want?
BRUYANT I want him to feel
    a little how much my hand weighs. 20,868
MALCUIDANT By God's shoes, what a bruiser!
    No blow was ever better dealt.
BRUYANT Should I give him six such,
    six like that for lunch? 20,872
DRAGON We could give him a good lunch
    of better meat to chew.
GUEULU Hey! Bruyant, you're not keeping order;
    you're going somewhat too fast. 20,876
ESTONNÉ Right again, and his paw is
    as hard as an iron hammer.
DRAGON It's the paw of a devil from hell.
    It breaks everything it touches. 20,880
GUEULU This villain is completely pale
    and his face all disfigured.
    For all the pain and beating,
    he neither grumbles nor complains. 20,884
CAIAPHAS What are you doing, Malcuidant?
BRUYANT He's hesitating.
    I think he's quitting the game.
MALCUIDANT May God send you misfortune.
    Are you going to give me that refrain? 20,888
ESTONNÉ This villain is completely pale,
    and his face all disfigured.
DRAGON His snout is too well imprinted
    with the many strokes visible on it. 20,892
GUEULU That didn't happen without giving him bruises.
    He is being very severely chastised.
JEROBOAM What is Estonné doing?
MALCUIDANT He's hesitating.
    I think he is quitting the game. 20,896
ESTONNÉ May God send you misfortune!

20,862 *je luy asseray ceste prune.* Literally, "I will give him this plum."

Are you going to give me that refrain?
BRUYANT His face is so pale,
    so swollen, and so full   20,900
    that he looks like a rotting leper
    because he is ugly and disfigured.
ESTONNÉ He's horribly scarred.
    I feel great horror in looking at him.   20,904
MALCUIDANT This response should be corrected.
    Estonné, aren't you any smarter?
ESTONNÉ What?
MALCUIDANT Let's cover his face,
    so that he can't see at all   20,908
    and then, I know a really good game
    that'll keep us busy.
ESTONNÉ What game is it?
MALCUIDANT We'll strike °
    his head until it's broken.   20,912
    Then we'll make him guess
    who gave him the blow.
    Do you agree to it?
ESTONNÉ Count me in.
    I like it. Now see   20,916
    if his eyes are well covered;
    Neither his nose nor his chin is visible.
DRAGON That's well said. There, let's turn him around.
    All we need to do is to strike him.   20,920
GUEULU Now, Jesus, guess
    who gave you this token.
BRUYANT I'll swear he got a good one.
    You've made his head ring. °   20,924
GUEULU He can't find the means.
    He's lost his skill.
ESTONNÉ No, he hasn't, it's just all gone down
    to his heel, °   20,928
    so that when the need arises
    he can't use it at all.
MALCUIDANT Guess now
    who gave you this whack.   20,932

20,911–950 The game of blindman's buff occurs in Matthew 26:67–68; Mark 14:65; Luke 22:63–65.
20,924 *tu as fait la cloche lever.* Literally, "you made the bell ring."
20,928 Christ's skill has descended into his heel, that is, it has disappeared.

DRAGON You are so wise and able,
　　　guess now.
GUEULU I'll know immediately
　　　if his sense is worth a leek.　　　　　　　　　　20,936
　　　Guess now
　　　who gave you this whack.
BRUYANT He is daydreaming.
　　　Our actions seem nothing but trifles to him.　　20,940
　　　Let's rouse him!
ESTONNÉ With what?
BRUYANT With slaps.
MALCUIDANT To flatten out his fat cheeks,
　　　let's rouse him.　　　　　　　　　　　　　　　20,944
DRAGON With what?
MALCUIDANT With slaps.
DRAGON Hey! Malcuidant, you're fooling yourself,
　　　you don't make your blows ring at all.
　　　Let's rouse him!
GUEULU With what?
DRAGON With slaps,
　　　given with all our might.　　　　　　　　　　　20,948
MALCUIDANT Take that and that!
BRUYANT Take that and that. Go preach
　　　and then call yourself Christ!
CAIAPHAS Whoa, friends, that's enough.
　　　Quickly stop this fighting.　　　　　　　　　　20,952
　　　What you do is only for amusement.
　　　This court of justice must be abridged,
　　　and we must execute his death as quickly
　　　as we can; this is our intention.　　　　　　　　20,956
　　　Beating him does not satisfy us
　　　if it is not followed by his death.
JEROBOAM As long as he is alive on earth,
　　　there will be no joy in our hearts.　　　　　　　20,960
CAIAPHAS Jewish lords, what do you say
　　　of this wretched deceiver?
　　　Do you not have a good guide
　　　and a worthy teacher?　　　　　　　　　　　　20,964
　　　You see the miserable end
　　　to which he must be led.
SALMANASAR He is an evil, crazed man.
　　　Put him to death no matter what that entails.　20,968
PHARÉS The people are really agitated.
　　　Prevent him from ever returning.

NENBROTH He destroys and obstructs the law.
　　He wants to feed us with his error.　　　　　20,972
EMILIUS So goes he who conducts himself so;
　　sin breaks its master's neck. °
CAIAPHAS Judging by what we hear from you
　　my good citizens and friends,　　　　　　　20,976
　　you all consent that he be put
　　into the hands of Pontius Pilate.
CELSIDON Not a soul contests it.
　　Let us make a mighty appeal against him　　20,980
　　so that we get our revenge of him
　　for all the evils he brought upon us.
CAIAPHAS It will be done. Do not doubt it,
　　and you will have him completely at your will,　20,984
　　for I never wished nor wish
　　to oppose your desire.
　　Soldiers, quickly seize
　　this evildoer here by the cloak　　　　　　20,988
　　and make sure that he does not escape from you,
　　on pain of being shackled.
BRUYART What will we do with him?
CAIAPHAS You will bring him
　　after us. Must you be told?　　　　　　　20,992
ESTONNÉ Our master is consumed with anger;
　　I don't know what the devil he wants.
MALCUIDANT It's because of this villain.
　　May God give him a bloody awful year!　　20,996
CAIAPHAS Naason and you, Jeroboam,
　　Elyachim, Bannanias,
　　Jacob, Isacar, Pelias
　　Nachor, Mardocee, Nathan,　　　　　　　21,000
　　Joram, sir, and you Joathan,
　　please, out of courtesy,
　　come keep me company
　　while finishing this business,　　　　　　21,004
　　for I dread terribly
　　that it will not be to our honor.
JEROBOAM Most high priest and perfect lord,
　　at your command we will do it　　　　　　21,008
　　and will be very happy
　　if your wishes are fulfilled.

20,974 *pechié rompt le col a son maistre.* A proverb (Jodogne, 448).

But here is my opinion.
Annas, your predecessor, °   21,012
is a high and loyal judge
who has seen many trials
and immense and terrible events:
it would be good for him to go with us   21,016
so that he can lend a hand
when it comes time to accuse him.
CAIAPHAS We could not plan it any better.
He is very honorable and old;   21,020
therefore, the judge will more readily believe us
when he hears our story.
Maucourant!
MAUCOURANT Sir.
CAIAPHAS You must go
promptly to seek Annas   21,024
and tell him that at this moment
he should present himself, rapidly and quickly,
at the house of Pilate, the governor,
and that on account of the case, which he knows about, 21,028
he will find there more than seven
of us awaiting his arrival.
MAUCOURANT If my task is achieved,
you will soon hear news of it.   21,032
We certainly encounter trouble and grief
in serving these lords like this!
Because they have so few cares,
we servants do nothing but fritter our time away.   21,036
CAIAPHAS It is time for us to go.
The governor has arisen, I think.
Lords, let us get ready.
Let us always go forward.   21,040
Lords, make this evildoer
walk forth; do you understand me?
And all of you, follow us
without saying anything; it is not the right moment.   21,044
MAUCOURANT I think this is the house
where Annas lives.
It's time that I tell him
my message, without further ado.   21,048

21,012 John 18:13 specifies that Annas is father-in-law to Caiaphas, a relationship
Gréban omits.

Sir, may god watch over you
and protect your body from harm!
The great sacerdotal prince
accompanied by citizens,   21,052
Scribes, and Pharisees
begs you to tarry no longer
and to present yourself immediately
before Pilate, the great judge.   21,056
ANNAS What are they doing there?
MAUCOURANT They are seeking support
    against this scoundrel.
ANNAS Oh, I understand.
    This is the thing I strive for
    more than anything else in the world.   21,060
MAUCOURANT It doesn't matter to me how things go.
    Then they told me
    that you will certainly find them there.
    Therefore please come   21,064
    and hurry up.
ANNAS I am ready.
    Come, servants, take these sticks.
    We must bestir ourselves
    and go quickly and fast   21,068
    to the criminal procurator.
    I think we are being summoned there.
ROILLART Your being called to the assembly
    is the sign of a trap.   21,072
    They boldly brought
    this libertine there in secret.
DENTART May the bloody gibbet play its part.
    We're having a lot of trouble for it.   21,076
JUDAS There is my master who is being taken away, °

21,077–138; 21,365–988 See Matthew 27:3–10. There are several differences between Marcadé's and Gréban's version of the Judas story:
  1. In Marcadé, Judas asks the Pharisees to return Christ. In Gréban, he
      does not.
  2. In Marcadé, Judas returns the money while the Pharisees confer with
      Pilate, and they inform him of Judas' betrayal of Christ. In Gréban, Pi-
      late is absent from this scene since it occurs after the Pharisees have left
      his court.
  3. In Marcadé, Judas calls on the devils who never actually speak to him.
      Two come forth and simply give him a noose. In Gréban, Judas has a
      long conversation with Despair, Lucifer's daughter. His suicide serves
      as a miniature morality play on the sin of despair.

treated quite pitiably;
it seems that his case
will end pitifully 21,080
and that death will follow.
There is no solution to his situation.
O evil murderer, what have you done?
Disloyal heart, what have you conspired? 21,084
Why did you dishonor yourself?
Whom did you attack?
You undertook
so great an outrage 21,088
that you will never be absolved
nor will the innocent one ever be compensated.
With my evil and terrible heart
that never wanted to conceive good 21,092
I committed the most horrible crime
that eyes ever did see.
Through fraud I deceived
the just and peaceful innocent one, 21,096
and I think it impossible for me
ever to receive pardon.
Holy man, just and zealous,
Jesus, in whom all good is embodied, 21,100
I was of your people
once, and I cleaved to you all;
and now, for a sum
of evil money 21,104
my perverse and disdainful heart
sold you; it is a great wrong.
Cursed and perverse money,
what mouth will curse you enough? 21,108
Cause of sorrow and hatred
in which there is much to curse.
Cursed be the slave of Fortune
who took you from the earth 21,112

---

4. Marcadé follows biblical order and has the Jews buy the Field of Blood
   after Judas' hanging (Matthew 27:3–10). Gréban reverses the order.
5. The above scenes occur without interruption in Marcadé (lines 12,978–
   13,215). In Gréban, the scenes are interwoven with events at Pilate's
   court and the Virgin's response to her son's arrest.
6. In Gréban's Second Day, Judas delivers a monologue in which he reveals that he has killed his father and married his mother. In Marcadé,
   these Oedipal allusions are lacking.

because on account of you, sorrow so afflicts me
that it will never leave me!
O master of true doctrine,
I once was in your school   21,116
of noble precepts
not to be refuted.
My participation there was a great evil.
I am not worthy of it   21,120
when by my wicked betrayal
I depart sorrowful and distraught.
Ah, hot brazier of covetousness,
more burning than iron-brands,   21,124
which stirs up and sets human hearts aflame
with sparks of hell's fire,
with what ardor you inflamed
my will to annihilate him!   21,128
You drew me into the region
of hell to live in without end.
I feel horror in possessing you,
false wretched money.   21,132
You made me do the work of the devil
of which I will never be acquitted.
Therefore I will return you
to those who gave you to me as a dower   21,136
and who provided me with the motives
for which I will find myself condemned.

Here Judas goes to return the money.
Likewise Saint John comes to Our Lady and says

SAINT JOHN My mistress, I will tell you °
news of bad events,   21,140
and it weighs on me that I must be
the bearer of it.
Our master is in great danger;
those traitorous Jews hold him   21,144
in their hands, some of whom claim
that they have condemned him to death.

21,139–264 In Marcadé, John first tells Mary of Christ's arrest after the scene at
Herod's court. On hearing the news, Mary faints twice and abuses the Jews
several times (lines 13,813–916). In Gréban, Mary asks God to find another means
for salvation, a scene that occurs in *Meditations on the Life of Christ* (Chapter 75).
Gabriel comforts her only in Gréban.

OUR LADY Oh, John, my well beloved nephew,
   do you know this to be true?   21,148
SAINT JOHN Yes my lady, I was
   in his company all the time
   until the traitors
   came to seize him in the garden   21,152
   to which Judas pointed out the path.
   And then, we who were there,
   because we feared death too much,
   took flight,   21,156
   seeing that we could not resist
   such a strong escort.
   They went on to present him
   before Annas, the former high priest;   21,160
   then they brought him to Caiaphas,
   where, as is told, he suffered
   much pain and humiliation
   without defending himself on any counts. 21,164
   And now I have heard
   that in great fury, they bring him
   to the emperor's governor
   to see him dishonorably murdered.   21,168
OUR LADY This most distressing news
   weighs on my heart so heavily
   that there is no means of consolation
   other than praying   21,172
   before the ineffable light
   that it may save me
   and protect my dear child.
   O glorious god,   21,176
   merciful father,
   O divine essence,
   who, from your gentle clemency,
   gave and bestowed on me   21,180
   a son so blessed,
   a son so precious,
   of such distinction
   that he is an incommensurate goodness 21,184
   completely in accord with you.
   Since he was in the heavens,
   before becoming mortal,
   I have the firm belief   21,188
   that he was wholly in your presence
   without being given to me.

But you have done something better for me,
for my good fortune is such 21,192
that I share in this.
I ask you for his defense
insofar as it is allowed me.
When I won such grace from you, 21,196
it was through your divine goodness
that I acquired this noble son
who is yours for all time.
I say that I was born fortunate 21,200
to have a son of such noble character.
Father, I never asked him of you.
I never thought myself worthy.
Therefore, my divine father, 21,204
who gave me, without my asking,
this sweet, good, and
truly obedient son,
return him to me at my request 21,208
so that he will always be near me
until the end;
this is my petition.
I seek no other advantage, 21,212
I have neither treasure nor goods
other than the one
who yields to your commands.
Therefore I commend him unto you; 21,216
otherwise his death is imminent
O triumphant father of heaven,
may you protect my son today
from these harsh and wicked people, 21,220
and if human salvation
can be achieved by another means,
your gentle grace can see to it,
since it is in your power. 21,224
Because your son wishes to continue
in noble obedience to you,
he does not try to defend himself
from the people who attacked him. 21,228
My most loving God, see to it
by more advantageous means.
GABRIEL Noble and reverent mistress,
for God's sake console yourself 21,232
and bear everything patiently.
As for the matter concerning the Blessed Savior,

your son and our lord,
he has said to you in the past 21,236
that he must, in cruel opposition,
give himself to death
to deliver the human race.
Therefore, you cannot 21,240
obtain your request.
But you can receive great comfort
from me, for I will do my duty
towards you and will comfort you 21,244
in your sorrows, which I can do,
and I will be your guardian.
OUR LADY Gabriel, my dear protector,
I do not doubt this at all. 21,248
Magdalene, my dear friend,
and you, my good and lovely sisters,
have you heard this news
which grieves my heart greatly 21,252
What do you think? What will we do?
Will we allow my dear son to die
without assisting or helping him
in his very bitter Passion? 21,256
Accompany the sorrowing mother,
who in her anguish does not know where to turn.
MAGDALENE I could not allow
you to go without me. 21,260
MARY JACOBI I will follow you everywhere
and will not leave you, come what may.
MARY SALOME May the grace of God come upon us
and guide us very well. 21,264

Here they go towards Pilate's court

CAIAPHAS Barraquin, you must guide
the way skillfully and quickly.
BARRAQUIN *Pilate's Usher*
What do you want?
CAIAPHAS Is not my lord Pilate
here, so 21,268
we can say a word
or two to him?
BARRAQUIN You're painfully early,
but what business draws you 21,272
now?
ANNAS We want him to attend to

a judicial process
which falls under his office.
Now, go get him right away.   21,276
BARRAQUIN I think he's still in bed
in order to avoid quarrels.
CAIAPHAS Tell him that the case is urgent
and falls well within his jurisdiction.   21,280
BARRAQUIN I don't know if he'll hurry,
but I'll tell him without delay.
My lord, may Mars and the great goddess Venus
grant you a good day!   21,284
All these Jews have come here
and their sacerdotal princes
who are more puffed up than toads; °
I don't know what to say.   21,288
PILATE *governor of Jerusalem*
Is that a way to talk, my good man?
You show that you know little.
If you had been smart
you would have gained us some advantage.   21,292
Now, go tell them for me
that I will come right away.
BARRAQUIN From what I see, I think
they're here for a very important case.   21,296
PILATE Do not worry why they are here,
tell them only that I am coming.
Above all else, let
my throne be richly decorated.   21,300
Put as many tapestries there
as you know will look good.
BARRAQUIN I understand your words very well.
Come, you will find everything ready.   21,304
Lords, please wait
a little, for it is necessary.
Here is my lord; he will come
as soon as he attires himself.   21,308
If you feel uncomfortable out there,
why don't you enter the praetorium?
MARDOCEE It is known in our law °
and we have rules   21,312

21,287 *Enflé comme un crappaud.* A proverbial phrase (Hassell, 86).
21,311–16 John 18:28.

~ 41 ~

which forbid us to do that,
for this night we must eat
the paschal lamb; there is the danger
that for this we will be polluted.   21,316
PILATE Lords, may the God you worship grant you
honor and salvation.
Whom do you bring me
now, in such haste?   21,320
Is he an evildoer or what?
What accusations, in short, °
do you bring against this man?
With what crimes do you charge him?   21,324
ANNAS You may be sure
that if he were not a great evildoer
and a perpetrator of great evils
we would not have troubled ourselves   21,328
in putting him into your hands.
There is more reason than you think.
CAIAPHAS Judge, you can understand well enough that
we would not have brought here
this man of false mintage,   21,332
cursed by God and the law,
without his being well questioned
with very thorough questions,   21,336
as much as our law permits;
and we have taken great care
to examine his offense.
We find him truly worthy of death,   21,340
but because we do not have the power
to kill and execute him,
maxime to crucify him, °
which act we absolutely demand,   21,344
we deliver and give him to you
to sentence him for his crime.
PILATE If he has broken your law °
and committed several crimes,   21,348
why do you not take him yourself
and judge him by your law?
JEROBOAM We want you to kill him,

21,322–30 John 18:29–30.
21,343 *maxime,* "especially."
21,347–54 John 18:31; *Passion d'Arras* (lines 13,557–64).

for as our master tells you,   21,352
the death we want for him
does not fall within our judicial power.
PILATE Give me, then, a report of
    the wickedness he engaged in.   21,356
    To issue a decree at your request
    is not my intention.
CAIAPHAS We bring a solid accusation,
    certain and proved.   21,360
    First, we found him °
    subverting our people
    and falsely perverting
    our forefathers' traditions,   21,364
    preaching and sermonizing against them,
    gathering families and households
    who want to oppose and destroy
    our sacred rituals.   21,368
    Second, he wants to lead
    the people through other falsehoods
    to pay none of the taxes
    that are due in very large sums   21,372
    to Caesar, the emperor of Rome;
    he says that the Jews are free
    and that we suffer Caesar unjustly.
    Third, which is even worse,   21,376
    he calls himself king of the Jews
    which by reason he should not and cannot do.
    If he wishes to deny these charges,
    we offer as proof   21,380
    an excellent preliminary investigation
    all confirmed by witnesses.

    [*Here he shows a scroll.*]

PILATE No matter what there is on the first two points,
    the third which you have named   21,384
    is a crime against the sovereign,
    because the emperor of the Romans,
    my master under whom I live,
    dissolved as a kingdom   21,388
    the whole land of Judea
    and divided it into three parts

21,361–378 Luke 23:2.

which form three tetrarchies.   21,392
When he divided it in this manner,
he decreed that whoever would call himself
king in this region
would quickly be punished by death.
Therefore I want to stop   21,396
on this point to inquire
if he has this presumption.

[*Pilate has Christ approach him. Note that in Pilate's praetorium
there are two seats, one higher than the other. Pilate sits in the lower
when conducting his interrogation and only sits in the higher when
sentencing Christ. Note that only Pilate enters this tribunal and that
Christ stands alone before him. The Jews remain outside.*]

Man of frail condition
you must be heard   21,400
Do you call yourself king of the Jews? °
Do you usurp the name of king?
JESUS Do you ask this of your own
or did others tell you this of me?   21,404
PILATE How could I speak of you?
I am not of these parts;
therefore, I know nothing about you
if you or others don't tell me.   21,408
If you preach or corrupt,
if you have worked evil or good
you must understand that I know nothing of this.
I am not a Jew by birth;   21,412
what I say is at the insistence
of the chief priests and the people
who publicly accuse you
of being a treacherous evildoer   21,416
and usurper of the royal name.
I do not know if such a grand title
applies to you; I think not.
My inquiry begins here.   21,420
JESUS My kingdom is not of this world.
If my powers were here,
my ministers would fight
so that the Jews would not have   21,424
license to keep me.

21,401–37 John 18:33–38; *Passion d'Arras* (lines 13,566–600).

PILATE So are you king?
    If one gleans your words well,
    it follows that you call yourself a king.
JESUS You say it
    and have given me the name of king.   21,428
    I was born into the world for this,
    to bear through all my words
    true witness to the truth.
    All true agents of humanity   21,432
    who uphold the way of truth
    gladly listen to my voice.
PILATE Since you know the truth
    and since you have reflected so deeply,   21,436
    good sir, *quid est veritas*? °

       Pilate rises, hastens outside, and says to the Jews

Jewish lords and governors,
who, to punish your evildoers,
have appointed me judge,   21,440
I have interrogated this poor man,
whose death you requested,
on his actions as best as I could.   21,444
But I do not find him
at all guilty of the sins
of which you accuse him and for which you detain him.
He seems a good person,   21,448
and I think you would do a kindness
to leave him as he is.
If his life displeases you too much,
let him be banished for his trespass.   21,452
CAIAPHAS Ah, governor, this is not sufficient;
    it is not a solution.
    He caused a great stir
    in order to promote himself as king.   21,456
    He excited the people
    and through great quarrels divided them,
    from the land of Galilee
    even to here, which wounds us very deeply.   21,460
    He is a man worthy of death,
    treacherous and suspect,

21,437 *quid est veritas?* John 18:38, "What is truth?" Marcadé rarely uses Latin and does not use it here. Gréban does so much more frequently.

a seeker of seditious means,
a mystifier, a quarreller, and a schismatic.   21,464
It will be against the public good
if he escapes in this way.
PILATE Since he is Galilean °
    insofar as he affects that region,   21,468
it is up to Herod, the tetrarch.
The case in no way concerns me.
But to fulfill my duty
and show that I bear you love,   21,472
I will very gladly send him forth,
charged with all these crimes,
so that Herod may judge
whether he deserves torture or death.   21,476
JEROBOAM You have power over his death and life.
    Aren't you the procurator appointed
to punish all enemies
of the emperor? Therefore, since we find   21,480
this man to be false and prove it
sufficiently, I do not see the reason
why it is necessary to make this referral.
It seems to me that this is an indefinite   21,484
    postponement.
PILATE As for me, I withdraw from the case,
    whether it is in my power or not in my power.
Herod is sufficiently qualified
to give him punishment;   21,488
it is in his jurisdiction,
and I will not oppose him at all.
Barraquin, call my servants;
make them hurry here.   21,492
BARRAQUIN Let them wake up first,
    for they are still in bed.
PILATE I believe you; it is their habit
to sleep all morning.   21,496
BARRAQUIN Griffon!
GRIFFON, *a Torturer*
    I hear you.
BARRAQUIN May Tervagant send you °

21,467–69 Luke 23:6–7. In Luke, Pilate asks if Jesus is Galilean; in Gréban, he does not.
21,498 Tervagant. The name of a god believed by medieval Europeans to be

~ 46 ~

a bad day.
Here roams my lord,
as lonely as an old dog, 21,500
and you're sleeping!
GRIFFON I believe so.
Am I too unimportant to do that?
BARRAQUIN Claquedent!
CLAQUEDENT, *Second Torturer*
Okay, I'm coming. I'm coming.
BARRAQUIN And you're sleeping? 21,504
CLAQUEDENT I believe so.
Don't worry. It's not your concern.
Don't I know my own business?
BARRAQUIN Orillart!
ORILLART, *Third Torturer*
What are you squawking about?
BARRAQUIN My lord calls you. Tisk, tisk. 21,508
and you're sleeping!
ORILLART I believe so.
Am I too unimportant to do that?
BARRAQUIN Brayart, are you being arrogant?
Will you come speak to the governor? 21,512
BRAYART, *Fourth Torturer*
To get a slice of the action?
My mouth is watering.
BARRAQUIN Here are really honest servants!
Look here, may God help you! 21,516
What courtly squires!
It seems they were born for it.
GRIFFON Go, go shit on your nose!
Are you making fun of us guys? 21,520
Where are we going?
Don't speak to us like good-for-nothings.
BARRAQUIN It is my lord who asks for you,
didn't I tell you? 21,524
GRIFFON My lord *proposite*, °
bona dies this morning. °
PILATE Say there, you speak Latin well,

---

worshipped by the Saracens (Jodogne, 362).
21,525 *proposite*. Variant or corruption of *preposite*, which is Latin for *prevost*, the
title that Greban gives to Pilate.
21,526 *bona dies*, "good day."

master Griffes. They are lovely words. 21,528
Come come, let's listen to what's being said.
It's not the time to chatter.
Carry out my will
in the manner told to you. 21,532
CLAQUEDENT None of us will oppose it
whether good or bad, sir governor.
PILATE You are a good one Claquedent.
Never did such a fool come forth. 21,536
Take this scoundrel
in the condition you see him
and quickly convey him
to Herod and all his lords. 21,540
Lead him and make sure
that he doesn't escape by some means.
Tell Herod that I send him
as a subject of his justice, 21,544
so that he may judge him
according to his investigation.
GRIFFON My lord, we will do
exactly as you wish. 21,548
Claquedent, take the other side,
and let's bring him in our own fashion.
CLAQUEDENT Where can we find Herod,
to whom he must be presented? 21,552
PILATE He came to the city °
to see the solemn feast.
BRAYART We will hear good news;
I know where he's staying. 21,556
ORILLART Now, let's hurry;
We can't have any delay.
Drive this hypocrite ahead;
be quick, it's high time. 21,560
ANNAS Lords, since we are not doing anything,
we should withdraw to the temple.
CAIAPHAS We do not have any objections.
We have a lot to do there. 21,564
JUDAS Ah, traitorous and lying heart,
what treason have you devised!
How did you so corrupt

21,553 The explanation for Herod's being in town has its source in Nicholas of
Lyra (Roy, 228).

your conscience, for profit, 21,568
as to trick and betray
the one who considered you his follower?
Alas, was it necessary?
Alas he had provided you with goods, 21,572
as much as or more than all his disciples.
How did you not have enough?
All this passed through your hands.
The others had none of it, 21,576
except on your orders.
In your misery and misfortune
you sold him to the false dogs
who seek only his torment! 21,580
Money of bad acquaintance,
money fashioned in misfortune,
money defiled with blood,
which burdened me with treason. 21,584
Cursed be he who forged you
and he who discovered the manner of doing so;
and cursed be the miner,
the earth, and the place where you increased 21,588
and the hour when I trusted in you!
O what horror has come upon me!
O in what port have I arrived!
O depraved money, 21,592
the horror of you drowns my heart.
You are the price of so high a crime
that I hardly dare look upon you.
Can I then find rest 21,596
by holding or possessing you?
No. The crime of holding you
will banish me from this world
and send me with the devil 21,600
to the bottom of eternal hell.
I am waiting only for the hour to come.
Money, may I never hold you!
Money, may I never see you, 21,604
since you directed me to the path
of eternal damnation!
I see the congregation
of false Jews; may God curse them. 21,608
I'll certainly have the nerve
to bring it back in one pile
to the false murderers who deceived me

and who are the cause of my fate.   21,612
Here lords, take your money!
Peccavi, alas, I have sinned °
and have committed such an enormous sin
that it is the cause of my destruction.   21,616
ANNAS *Quid ad nos?* °
CAIAPHAS But what does it matter to us?
If you transgressed on your own
or acted rashly, then take the consequences;
your action affects only you.   21,620
Do you understand? It's of no concern to us,
nor should you matter to us.
JUDAS Ah, people of terrifying resolve
I delivered into your hands   21,624
the most just blood among all humans;
and if he must meet with death,
it is my fault.
ANNAS May it serve you right.
Make the best of it that you can.   21,628
You will receive no other comfort from us.
If you have done well, good for you;
if badly, may evil dwell with you,
and may you fall into filth.   21,632
JUDAS Alas, here is a harsh response!
Those whom I greatly pleased
are happy at my displeasure,
nor does my chagrin matter to them.   21,636
Such is the end that comes of treason,
for when a traitor falls,
everyone laughs if misfortune befalls him.
My betrayal will finish badly,   21,640
for in the end misfortune will befall me.
I will leave here, for I grieve so much
that, if I stay even a little longer,
my heart will find itself so heavy   21,644
that it will burst from sorrow.
I will seek relief elsewhere.
MARDOCEE Lords, you witness the fact
that our money is returned to us.   21,648

21,614 *Peccavi.* Matthew 27:4, "I have sinned." Gréban often supplies translations
of Latin phrases within the same or the following line.
21,617 *Quid ad nos?* Matthew 27:4, "What is that to us?"

Let us now think of
finding the means and ways
of doing good with it,
for losing it would be improper.   21,652
NAASON My opinion is that,
given the situation we find ourselves in,
the money should not be put
in the treasury in which are the other gifts   21,656
that we give and donate to the temple.
Do I have a reason for this? Yes, I have,
because it paid for blood
and is the price of human death,   21,660
for which reasons the money is vile
and unworthy of so holy a place.
ELYACHIM We will never profit from it;
otherwise we would be dishonored.   21,664
But here is what we will do;
let us buy a field of land
where we will bury and inter
poor travelling pilgrims   21,668
dying on the road.
Once this purchase is completed,
the garden, for an appropriate reason,
will be named Haceldama. °   21,672
CAIAPHAS Your reasoning is good and sound,
and I'm with you on this.
BANNANIAS So are we all.
Judas is so agitated;   21,676
see how he threw
the money to the ground when returning it.
ANNAS However, it will not remain there.
It must be picked up and put aside,   21,680
until we can find
a merchant who will sell us a field.
JUDAS My soul is so tired of living
and bears my body like such a great burden   21,684
that it must disburden itself,
and only seeks the means to do so,
so that it can be rid of it.
Their very human friendship   21,688
once united by love,

21,672 Haceldama. Matthew 27:8, the "Field of Blood."

transforms itself into turmoil,
crying, and lamentation,
so much so that my soul hates its body   21,692
and the body hates the soul, and both have agreed
to make their separation,
villainously and disgracefully,
with pain, shame, and dishonor.   21,696
There only remains to find some soul
who will bring about the separation;
my soul would have already been gone
had it known to whom to turn,   21,700
one who could have helped it in this.
My soul, where can you search?
You can do no better than to invoke
all the damned devils of hell,   21,704
both demons and those born of Adam,
for if you turn to them,
do not doubt of receiving help.
There is nothing to do but to compel them   21,708
to come by calling them,
and here is the correct method:
Terrible deformed troops,
devils enclosed in the deep abyss,   21,712
false spirits deprived of glory,
cursed and wretched race,
damned under interminable pain
which can never finish you off,   21,716
come; advance forth!
Come, devils, come forward,
come help your servant,
who very loudly summons and calls you!   21,720
Come kill, destroy, and annihilate
this mortal substance,
or at least advise me
how I can be rid of it.   21,724
LUCIFER Devils listen, I will preach
a few pleasing words.
I think I heard
the voice of our servant,   21,728
Judas, the evil traitor,
cry out to death
because of the sin tormenting him,
but not a soul responds.   21,732
One after the other, he invokes us,

but we are not too distant
to aid him in his need.
He must be helped with all our might.   21,736
Leap forth Despair,
my daughter and well beloved child.
Go listen to my servant
who calls us so loudly   21,740
and give him what he needs
as you know how to do,
by which method you are accustomed
to bringing them back in droves.   21,744
DESPAIR Father Lucifer, if I fail,
I wish never to be seen here.
Villain, what do you want done to you?
What port do you wish to reach?   21,748
JUDAS I do not know. My eyes
dare not look at the heavens.
DESPAIR If you want to ask about my name,
you will soon know who I am.   21,752
JUDAS Where do you come from?
DESPAIR From the depths of hell.
JUDAS What is your name?
DESPAIR Despair.
JUDAS Terror of vengeance,
horror of enslavement,   21,756
approach and give me relief,
if death can relieve my suffering.
DESPAIR Yes. Very well.
JUDAS Approach then
and claim my cursed days.   21,760
DESPAIR I am ready without deceit
to end your case.
JUDAS Despair, horrible beast,
does my situation seem so terrible to you   21,764
that it holds my heart in its power?
DESPAIR It is quickly evident
that it is impossible
ever to obtain pardon for your sin.   21,768
JUDAS Alas, my master is so benevolent
and so inclined to forgive.
If I were to go to pray for mercy,
would he forgive me?   21,772
DESPAIR No,
for whoever acts with hidden venom

receives death as his reward.

JUDAS I never heard him preach
    other than to forgive, to forgive;   21,776
    it is a sign that he likes the offering.

DESPAIR As much as he may enjoin pardon,
    he can never give it to you.
    Betrayal receives no pardon.   21,780

JUDAS Alas, I have truly betrayed him
    and disobeyed his command,
    but pity is in his command.

DESPAIR But you are so hated by him   21,784
    that there was never a greater shame
    than for you to dare to be seen before him.

JUDAS It would seem then, if one listens to you,
    that he could not pardon me,   21,788
    he who has divine power.

DESPAIR I concede that he could indeed,
    but he would never consent to it.
    Why? Because you are not worthy of it.   21,792

JUDAS As for me, I argue yes
    and can be supported,
    for he often said
    that he came for the sinners;   21,796
    and if he descended for sinners
    and has known my sin,
    I will obtain his grace because
    he bestows it on all. He is bound to pardon.   21,800

DESPAIR Now let's suppose that, willingly,
    I admit your reason is good;
    there is a great range among sins:
    one is small, the other offends.   21,804
    There is none like yours,
    for it affects him too deeply;
    as a result, his doing good to others
    does not harm or help you.   21,808

JUDAS And when my soul seeking mercy
    approaches the sweet virgin Mary
    and depicts its pain to her,
    I suspect that   21,812
    she will obtain grace for me from her son,
    for she is his mother and friend;
    what a mother requests,
    a son never refuses.   21,816

DESPAIR You never have harbored such madness °
      if your will consents to this,
      for you slew mother and son.
      You will never appease   21,820
      this mother, who is mindful of your deed,
      by praying a hundred or a thousand times,
      for if someone wounds the son's body,
      the mother's heart feels it.   21,824
JUDAS You therefore reach the conclusion
      that I must be ravished by death.
      How so? I confessed,
      by saying *peccavi*.   21,828
      Then I made restitution
      by returning the money,
      and then felt such contrition
      that my heart almost burst.   21,832
DESPAIR You performed this confession
      without devout thought
      and restored all the money
      not to the offended party.   21,836
      In a gathering rage,
      you strove for the opposite.
      As a result, all that you cooked up
      amounts to nothing; time has run out. °   21,840
JUDAS And therefore, is my soul completely the devil's,
      left to its damnation?
DESPAIR It must be so.
JUDAS Damned to the eternal pit,
      without any possible remedy?   21,844
      Repressed redoubtable rage
      rendering redoubled reinforcements,
      rage, rage more enraging
      than the fury which rises in me!   21,848
      Death, death why do you hold me in suspense?
      Come soon, strike me with your arrow.
      I repent. I repent,
      and Despair taunts me.   21,852

21,817 Despair convinces Judas that Mary, the wounded mother, will not act as an intermediary in obtaining Christ's pardon. Judas then commits the sin of doubting not only Christ but also Mary. In the *Passion de Semur*, Mary herself tells Judas to ask Christ for mercy (lines 6,639–46).
21,840 *La fleur en est passee.* Literally, "The flower has passed away" or "faded."

DESPAIR Death need not yet strike
with her dart; put yourself under my protection.
And after, go hang yourself;
here is a rope I'm saving for you.   21,856
JUDAS Alas, will I die in such a manner,
strangled by a noose
without any hope of solace?
O Despair, alas,   21,860
you hold the cell
into which death wants to draw me!
All kinds of pain
seek me in great number.   21,864
Covetousness, you are very wrong
to have brought to me and shown me
the means
for which I suffer such misfortune.   21,868
Alas, what must I do?
Must I kill myself?
Is this death necessary?
Pity, are you against me,   21,872
you who should
rather pardon my offense?
DESPAIR This bawling doesn't do any good,
nor does retreating to mercy.   21,876
Go away, quickly, plan your death
of your own free will,
do it and shut up.
You must take this step.   21,880
JUDAS How?
DESPAIR Don't worry.
I will certainly show you the methods.
Now look at my instruments here,
see if I am not provided with the clever tools   21,884
belonging to my trade.
I have my razor, my huge knife;
there is none that is not from a good forge,
very sharp and excellent   21,888
for immediately slitting your throat.
If you need daggers or poignards,
I have several kinds.
Stick this one hard into your belly   21,892
tightly down to the handle.
Here are ropes, cords, and chains
which I prepare for friends

to strangle themselves quickly. 21,896
    Choose fast. You linger too long.
    Strike while the iron is hot.
JUDAS Since I must despair
    and be deprived of all hope, 21,900
    and since I lack the gift of hope,
    I no longer need assurance.
    Kill me Despair.
    It's time that you attend to my death. 21,904
DESPAIR Which death best suits your liking?
JUDAS I ask that you hang me.
DESPAIR To that end, so that you don't wait too long,
    I'll carry this rope, 21,908
    and you will hang yourself.
    It's the best thing you can do.
    But I will gladly help you
    to dispatch yourself as quickly as possible. 21,912
JUDAS Let's go then, I ask that we hurry
    or my heart will burst with rage.
    On which gibbet will I hang myself?
    Despair, what do you think? 21,916
DESPAIR Here is an old gnarled elder tree
    with many branches.
    It will hold you securely.
    Climb on it, and I will help you. 21,920
JUDAS I will hang myself on this one here
    and will strangle myself by the neck,
    but first, I will tie this rope
    to make it quick. 21,924
DESPAIR Is it done well?
JUDAS Ah noose, you are
    strong enough to bear my weight.
    Horrible and wretched devils,
    villainous and condemned troop, 21,928
    vile and cursed company
    eternally in hell,
    I make no testament other
    than to give up my body and soul to you 21,932
    in the eternal flame.
    To you I yield, to you I give myself,
    to you do I bind and surrender myself,
    without hope of ever escaping. 21,936
BERICH So that I may not be tricked,
    I'm happy to be the notary public

to write this worthy testament.
Here is my paper, ready to go.   21,940
JUDAS O grievous burden
of rage that carries off my heart,
must I henceforth bear you
in eternal affliction?   21,944
High tower of Despair,
fortified with piteous cries,
covered in pitiful lamentation,
enclosed by an eternal wall   21,948
made and forged by a devil's hand,
hollowed out by deep wells
and abysses without borders or bottom,
where, alas, the rooms have   21,952
only snares for comfort,
wait for me terrible dwelling;
in you I will dwell.
Wait for me most horrible pit,   21,956
for I will endlessly die a painful death
in the eternal brimstone.
Wait for me, dolorous prison,
red furnace of burning fire,   21,960
ditch of myriad serpents,
river of stinking mire;
to my grievous pain and distress,
I will plunge into you.   21,964
But on parting I cry out loud:
devils, whose commands I obeyed,
I commend my soul and body to you.

Here Judas hangs himself

BERICH Despair, dear sister,   21,968
is he dead?
DESPAIR I'm waiting until his heart
bursts and splits in the middle
and then he will soon issue forth,
he will come out little by little.   21,972
BERICH I don't know what the devil's wrong.
I don't hear him breathe or cough
and, yet his soul
can't get out. But what's holding it back?   21,976
DESPAIR Ah hah, I know what's the matter.
When the villain broke his faith,
he came and kissed his master,

and through that malevolent mouth,   21,980
    which touched such a worthy being
    the soul must not nor cannot pass.
BERICH We must rip and split open his belly °
    and pull out all his guts,   21,984
    so he can give up his soul more easily.
    Do you want this done, my sister?
DESPAIR I consent.
    Let's hurry. I have our prey.
    There is nothing to do but depart.   21,988
OUR LADY O evil and felonious Jews,
    people banished from truth,
    where has my child been taken?
    Alas, in what place will I seek him?   21,992
    Alas, where will I find him?
    Alas, who will tell me any news?
    Evil and cruel race,
    why do you not now return to me
    my son, my joy, my treasure,   21,996
    whom I so love, and when I seek no other?
    Alas, I humbly ask you,
    very lovely daughters of Zion,   22,000
    that if someone speaks to you of him,
    please inform me of it.
MAGDALENE Some attest
    that he was brought a short while ago   22,004
    before Pilate, the procurator,
    who very cunningly
    abstained from judgment
    and, to better find the means of doing so,   22,008
    had him led back
    to Herod, the cruel pagan.
OUR LADY In the name of God, my dear friend,
    let us find a way to follow him,   22,012
    for I have absolutely no joy,
    if I do not know how he is.
MARY JACOBI Alas, the good Lord never did
    them wrong nor harmed them,   22,016
    and yet they torment him so,
    without having provided a reason.

21,983 The explanation for the disembowelment of Judas occurs in Peter Comestor's *Historia scolastica* (Combarieu du Grès and Subrenat, 516).

MARY SALOME They have long plotted
    his death and will never stop   22,020
    until they prevail.
    I ask God to watch over him.
OUR LADY Amen, my sisters. The time seems long
    until we hear news.   22,024
BERICH Devils, rejoice
    in joy mixed with rage
    and howl with great cries
    like old starving wolves. °   22,028
    Your servant, whom you so love,
    is coming quickly here
    to take possession of the gift
    with which you pay your lackeys.   22,032
LUCIFER Who is it, Berich?
BERICH It's Judas,
    that arrogant traitor.
LUCIFER Who's bringing him?
BERICH Despair.
    You'll soon hear the story.   22,036
DESPAIR Here he is, the evil traitor.
    Here he is, the false coveter.
    Here he is, the false, disloyal servant,
    quite pitiful, I think.   22,040
    Lucifer, my infernal father,
    I return him to you; I deliver him to you
    so that he may live endlessly in affliction
    as your captured subject.   22,044
LUCIFER I will not welcome him.
    Despair, dear daughter,
    you have proved to be clever.
    Now give him to me to touch,   22,048
    I want to swallow him quickly.
    Since I've got him in my paw,
    I want to gulp down the traitorous
    little thief in one piece.   22,052
ASTAROTH That's a devil of a gullet!
    Look how fast he's devoured him!
FERGALUS He has a bottomless pit,
    without bounds and immeasurable.   22,056
    He has such huge and wide jaws,

22,028 *vieulx loups tous affaméz*. Proverbial phrase (Hassell, 151).

that it looks like an old, gaping ruin.

CERBERUS Ten million damned souls inside it
　　amount to nothing more than a drop in a well.　　22,060
　　And their snouts are more cooked
　　and their brains more burnt
　　than if they had been a hundred years
　　inside a burning metal furnace.　　22,064

ASTAROTH Lucifer, poisonous old serpent,
　　you proud, detestable, and infamous king,
　　when you have done with his soul,
　　give it back to us quickly so that　　22,068
　　we can play with it a little
　　and amuse ourselves.

LUCIFER Here it is, my little dragons,
　　my young pupils,　　22,072
　　go play football with it
　　instead of hanging around the dunghill.

BERICH Since I should get the first kick,
　　you should give it to me.　　22,076

FERGALUS Oh yeah! Why?

BERICH I brought him here,
　　and I did all the work.

LUCIFER Listen to Berich's defense;
　　it's only right that he have his share.　　22,080

CERBERUS Damn it, he'll get nothing!
　　Your stinking talk is driving us crazy.

FERGALUS The first one to get it, kicks first;
　　to the first go the first blows.　　22,084
　　Isn't that the best way, Cerberus?
　　One mustn't play favorites.

CERBERUS It's the quickest way.

ASTAROTH It's the best.
　　Berich, you missed anyway.　　22,088
　　Come on devils, come on!

FERGALUS At'em! At'em!
　　It's time for the fun to start.

ASTAROTH Let's smash the traitor!
　　Come on devils, come on!　　22,092

BERICH At'em! At'em!

CERBERUS Since everyone else is joining in,
　　it's time for me to jump into the fight.
　　Come on, devils, come on! At'em!

ASTAROTH At'em!
　　It's time for the fun to start.　　22,096

LUCIFER You're making a frightful ruckus.
        Devils, do you have to howl so much?
        You're making all the infernal chasms
        bounce and shake.   22,100
        Stop, stop, stop, rogues!
        Do you want to kill our hireling?
FERGALUS No, we're just celebrating
        his gracious debut.   22,104
CERBERUS Let them carry on.
        Lucifer, give us your consent.
LUCIFER You've played one game too long.
        You'll have to amuse yourselves with another.   22,108
        Quickly seize him,
        bring him to execution
        in the slough of perdition
        and plunge him into the very bottom.   22,112
BERICH His arms will be thoroughly gnawed by
        serpents of many kinds.
        There are all sorts,
        more abundant than the mountains of Armenia. °   22,116
LUCIFER Go forth, foul troop,
        torment him for me.
ASTAROTH It would've been good if he had received
        a nice blessing on his arrival.   22,120
LUCIFER If my scheme hasn't failed
        and my hook isn't broken,
        he'll receive it. Corrupt servant,
        minister of betrayal,   22,124
        killed by desperation,
        deprived of grace and all hope,
        go to the place of despair,
        to the place of a harsh and vile death,   22,128
        to bear interminable pain
        and sorrow without hope of salvation;
        you will never leave the hopeless swamp
        for even a day of your life,
        but you will keep company and have kin   22,132
        among all the devils
        as long as God lasts without end!

22,116 *plus haut que les noms d'Armenie*. A typographical error in Jodogne's text
substitutes *noms* for *mons*. The 'mons d'Armenie' include Mount Ararat, where
Noah's ark is said to have rested. See correction in Jodogne's edition, II, 359.

BARRAQUIN Sire, tetrarch of great renown, °   22,136
    may Jupiter who governs the sky
    and makes it turn according to his will
    keep you from evil and suffering.
    Pilate, my master and lord,   22,140
    delegate of Caesar, the emperor,
    great governor of this city,
    sends you a new man
    in a novel circumstance.   22,144
HEROD Who is he? Let me see him!
    What has he done until now
    that Pilate gives him to me as a present?
    He must certainly be clever.   22,148
BARRAQUIN He calls himself Jesus.
    You will see him here right away.
HEROD Is it Jesus of Nazareth,
    who performs so many great miracles?   22,152
BARRAQUIN Yes, sire, I assure you,
    it is really he; you must not doubt it.
    And the better to present him to you,
    we have come in great number.   22,156
HEROD By my lady, saint Venus,
    to whom I owe faith and homage,
    notwithstanding the loss and harm
    which Pilate caused me in the past   22,160
    when he destroyed and killed my people, °
    I am happy for the present moment
    because of this man whom he presents to me.
    Bring him here before me.   22,164

[The torturers place Jesus all alone before Herod]

GRIFFON Barraquin, tell him why
    our procurator sent Jesus to him.
BARRAQUIN Sire, he has many enemies;
    the Pharisees strongly attack him   22,168
    and with all their might oppose

22,136–386 Only Luke 23:8–12 gives the account of Christ before Herod; see also *Passion d'Arras* (lines 13,685–812).

22,161–64 Neither Luke nor Marcadé offers an explanation for the previous enmity between Herod and Pilate. According to Roy (228), Gréban follows Nicholas of Lyra in having Herod refer to Pilate's having killed his people. In the *Passion Isabeau*, however, the narrator also mentions Pilate's having executed some men under Herod's jurisdiction.

his full release.
Pilate, knowing their attitude
and that the Jews object to him,   22,172
and are not authorized to condemn him,
and seeing that he is from your country,
is your subordinate and subject,
and wanting to be rid of him,   22,176
sends him to you to judge
if there is anything blameworthy in his actions.
HEROD By my faith, one could not speak better;
it is a sign of good will   22,180
that he entrusts us with the sentencing
and brings us honor and glory.
Jesus, to tell the truth, it seems to me
you were truly stupid   22,184
when you did not come see me in the past,
seeing that you are a native of my land
and that your youth flowered
in my land and state.   22,188
As a result, you must be more eager to
delight and gratify me,
and do things that please me.
Anyway, you have lived here   22,192
a long time,
and you have never visited nor come to
nor arrived at my court,
which seems disobedient.   22,196
Now, do you see that I have the power
to decide your life or your death?
Are you indeed under my rule?
You planned poorly   22,200
because I have desired for a long time
to see you and no other,
for you are the most renowned
of all those belonging to the empire.   22,204
Thus of two choices you chose the worse,
since you did not come to me.
Now tell me why this was so.
Speak, excuse yourself boldly,   22,208
and I will listen to you with kindness.
I rejoice over your good reputation,
for it is the honor of my country
and, consequently, of me as well.   22,212
What do you say? Won't you speak?

Make some response.
RADIGON I wonder if he bears you anger.
    It seems he doesn't respond at all.   22,216
JEROBOAM My lords, I have thought of a complication °
    that could soon harm us;
    you have seen that the procurator
    sent Jesus, that false and traitorous dog,   22,220
    to Herod
    to conduct his trial.
    We must fear methods
    that could be dangerous to us.   22,224
    Herod is very curious
    and strongly desires to hear
    novelties in order to rejoice,
    and he takes pleasure in seeing great signs   22,228
    performed through magic or divine works.
    Therefore, if it should happen that Jesus performs
    some marvel, Herod will favor him
    and maybe will find   22,232
    the means to free him.
    Thus we must oppose Jesus
    and accuse him ever more forcefully,
    so that he does not escape because of this.   22,236
MARDOCEE I am certainly in agreement with this;
    it is spoken by a crafty man.
ISACAR It is cleverly planned.
    Let's go to finish up our work.   22,240
JACOB We must work at it
    or our case is lost.
HEROD Come on, Jesus, why don't you respond?
    You must feel great shame.   22,244
    Is what is told to us
    about your deeds and feats true?
    It is said that you revive the dead.
    If you have undertaken such work,   22,248
    it is a miracle of great worth.
    Now then, tell me the truth,
    how many did you revive,
    where, and who were they?   22,252
AMPHIRARUS Your words do not concern him at all;

22,217–42 The Pharisees' worry over the possibility of Herod's favoring Christ
does not exist in the *Passion d'Arras*.

he does not answer with a word or a sound.

Pause

ABDALUS I don't understand what's happening. °
    I think he is sleeping or dozing.   22,256
GROIGNART Do you want me to wake him up
    with a well-placed blow?
HEROD Groignart, I prohibit laying hands on him.
    Don't touch him or you'll lose an eye.   22,260
GROIGNART Then where? On the nose?
HEROD I want
    you to leave him as he is.
GROIGNART This wicked villain so vexes me
    that he swells my heart with anger.   22,264
    We sue for his release,
    and he still does not deign to answer.
    May hell's fire destroy him!
    He is a rough villain.   22,268
HEROD You're awfully pensive;
    talk to me, I beg you.
RADIGON Leave off this melancholy
    and say something to my lord.   22,272
    You hear the horror they propose for you,
    from which he can easily deliver you.
GROIGNART Either he does not deign or does not want to;
    I have never seen such obstinacy.   22,276
    I would give him a good one
    if I had him under my rule.
HEROD Do you not know how to restore sight
    to the blind? It is a great thing.   22,280
    I ask you in order to do good,
    for I have many of them in my lands
    whom I would soon send for
    if you wanted to heal them,   22,284
    for it is a power without equal.
    If you have it, one must conclude
    that you are Jupiter or Mercury
    or one of the divine company;   22,288
    and you must be more inclined
    to heal a blind man
    in the land in which you were born

22,255 *Je n'entens point ceste leçon.* Literally, "I do not understand this lesson."

than to do works of such great importance   22,292
in other far away regions
from which you did not originate.
Moreover, you understand now
that those before whom you performed   22,296
such miracles and such noble deeds
are the ones who most strongly solicit me,
who want and seek your death.
Therefore, you have poorly employed   22,300
the good which you dispersed
among them in such great quantity
when they are not even grateful to you for it.
Perform some miracle before me;   22,304
just one would suffice,
provided it be really remarkable
and it may well be so brilliant
that I will release you.   22,308
RADIGON If ever a ponderer pondered,
he ponders long enough.
JEROBOAM Sire, do not attend to
these signs and obfuscations;   22,312
they are nothing but enchantments
caused by diabolical art.
MARDOCEE All that he concocts is by magic
and by invoking the devils,   22,316
who are so gracious to him
that they do whatever he asks.
HEROD Will you do nothing even if ordered?
Will you maintain this arrogance?   22,320
Good sir, if you have power,
give me here some signal
either by magic or miracle,
and I promise you by my faith   22,324
that I will work for you
against all your adversaries.

Pause

ELYACHIM As for him, he is rebellious and
obstinate in all his business,   22,328
and to villains from the countryside
he sooner shows his greatest signs
than he does to great lords.
He only pursues idleness and amusement.   22,332
Publicans, known sinners,

and foolish, licentious women:
those are the people he consorts with,
and that is what disturbs us.   22,336
HEROD Oh, now I see what he is!
He is nothing but a sot, a dreamer,
a hypocrite, a crazy idiot.
I suppose he is completely crazy.   22,340
And so is he nothing else?
I used to think, many years ago,
that he was a very saintly man,
one on whom had descended from the heavens   22,344
the might of one of our gods.
But I now perceive
that he has neither power nor strength
and that his actions are nothing but trickery.   22,348
Because of this I want him dressed in white
like an imbecile
and a really stubborn fool. °
I do not know of a garment better suited to him.   22,352
Groignart!
GROIGNART I understand perfectly, my lord;
you command that I dress him
in white like a stupid beast
having neither sense nor understanding.   22,356
HEROD Exactly. Take the clothing
of one of my most sottish fools
and put it on his naked body
as you know how to do.   22,360
GROIGNART You will wear a luxurious garment;
here is your perfect garb.

[*Here they put a white, mid-calf length fool's robe over his robe.*]

Look at his appearance.
He is such an obvious idiot;   20,364
I have never seen so stupid a snout.
My lord, look at his expression!
Is the garment suitable?
RADIGON It is worthy of him

22,351 The white robe is also mentioned by Nicholas of Lyra (Roy, 228). In
Gréban, Herod orders the white robe after addressing Christ five times without
receiving a response; in Marcadé, he does so after addressing him only once
(13,776).

and appropriately coarse. 20,368

GROIGNART He has a clownish head and clumsy fingers.
    Now if he'd just do something ridiculous,
    something really strange and surprising,
    we'd all die laughing. 22,372

HEROD Come on soldiers, take your fool!
    He is worthy of being led to pasture.
    You will bring him to your master
    in this white robe 22,376
    and tell him that I thank him
    for the great honor that he bestowed upon me
    and that all is forgiven him,
    whatever the harm he once did me, 22,380
    and we will be friends as before
    and will never have bad feelings.

BARRAQUIN We will accomplish your will
    with joyous hearts, sir tetrarch. 22,384
    May Juno, the beautiful goddess,
    keep you in her protection.

[They bring Jesus back to Pilate.]

OUR LADY My son, full of affection,
    my very sweet fruition, 22,388
    whom alone I desire,
    where are you, in what abode?
    Where do you dwell?
    Alas, I do not know where to search for you! 22,392

MAGDALENE May God come to your aid,
    my lady, let us press on.
    I see a great host of people
    and I think they are going to request 22,396
    Pilate, the procurator,
    to sentence him to death.

OUR LADY Alas, they will keep him concealed
    and will hide him so well 22,400
    that we will not be able to talk to him,
    for they will shut the door tightly
    and we will be left on the outside.

MARY JACOBI Let's follow them
    and stay near the gate. 22,404

BARRAQUIN My dear sir, we are quickly

returning our *magister* to you. °
PILATE Ah, cursed be Jupiter, °
    must I execute him?   22,408
    This was what I feared;
    and to rid myself of the whole problem,
    I wanted to send him away,
    and he is sent back to me.   22,412
GRIFFON To tell you the story briefly,
    no matter what Herod tried,
    he did not answer a word
    or make a sign or an utterance,   22,416
    and because of his foolish conduct
    Herod had him dressed so.
PILATE Argh, what vexation!
    I'm on the verge of exploding with rage!   22,420
BARRAQUIN And I forgot to tell you
    that Herod and all his family
    thank you a thousand times
    for the honor he sees in you   22,424
    and is very grateful
    and is your friend from this hour.
PILATE Is this true?
BARRAQUIN I assure you of it
    and if some harm befell you,   22,428
    Herod would be cursed if he did not come
    help you without being asked.
PILATE Argh, I cannot forget
    this villain although he did wrong.   22,432
    It does not matter to me what Herod would have done
    as long as I can be rid of Jesus,
    for my heart has always told me
    that in the end he will bring me great misfortune.   22,436
    Now then, lords, you need to
    temper your pursuit.
    You have been able to consider
    my situation and my resources.   22,440
    You have brought me this man
    charged with several crimes
    worthy of death, as you say,

22,406 *magister,* "ruler." Ironic.
22,407 Pilate in Marcadé expresses no displeasure at Christ's return and even
sends for Caiaphas to help him decide what to do about Christ.

as having greatly corrupted 22,444
your people and completely perverted them
and stirred up much evil.
And yet you have seen
that, with all my effort, 22,448
having summoned him in your presence,
entreated and examined him,
nevertheless, he did not reveal
anything prejudicial to himself 22,452
or for which imperial justice
should sentence him to death.

ANNAS One would never expect
him to confess anything 22,456
which could turn to his ruin.
He keeps quiet on anything that affects him,
for one must curse the mouth
that harms its body. 22,460
However, you must not delay
in judging him, you who are judge
and who, supplied with proof,
see the evil of your subjects. 22,464

PILATE As for the preliminary investigation, °
if I had conducted it alone,
then you could have said it was poorly done,
arguing favoritism in me. 22,468
But no, I did better;
I had him brought to Herod,
who is a wise man in rule
and still, from what I see, 22,470
he finds no cause any more than I do.
Reason agrees that this is true,
for Herod, of his own will, sent him back to me
as an innocent 22,474
to do with as I wish.
And since I don't see any grounds,
nor does Herod, nor the law, nor a statute

22,465–512 Luke 23:13–16; *Passion d'Arras* (lines 13,987–14,014). Following the biblical account, both Marcadé and Gréban have Pilate refuse to condemn Christ since Herod has found him innocent. While Marcadé's Pilate also fears possibly grave consequences, in Gréban's version he is worried about morality, stating that the gods and reason are against the condemnation (lines 22,483–84). Pilate then offers Barrabas. Marcadé, following biblical order, has Pilate first propose chastisement, and when this solution is rejected, he offers Barrabas (lines 14,055–76).

guiding the judge in passing sentence,   22,480
do you then want me to sentence him
to suffer death because of your words?
No, Reason opposes it
and likewise all our gods.   22,484
But, to take another approach,
I have found a good method
by which no man will be harmed
and with which we will keep to the middle path.   22,488
You have an ancient custom
that when I have several prisoners,
malefactors, thieves, or murderers
who must die because of their evil,   22,492
when your high Passover comes,
if I have two, three, or four of them,
you can select one of them,
the one you want freed,   22,496
and by this arrangement, he will be liberated
in sign of the deliverance
from Egypt which you received as a noble act,
as you know better than I;   22,500
you have it written in the law.
Now, there are in my prisons
several who for their wrongdoing
are worthy of death's assaulting them;   22,504
only sentencing remains.
Among them is one
who led a seditious rebellion
against the common good   22,508
and who is a murderer; he is Barrabas.
You know him; he's the only one.
Therefore I charge you to choose him
or Jesus who is called Christ.   22,512
CAIAPHAS We will reflect on this,
    and then you will hear our response.
PILATE Now be brief or I will announce
    that I seek a quick trial.   22,516
ANNAS Our suit proceeds well.
    There remains only to persuade
    all the people to demand
    Barrabas and to destroy Jesus.   22,520
CAIAPHAS We must instruct all the people
    to request him no matter what the result.
    Let's go to parents and cousins,

uncles, nieces, and nephews   22,524
and let us spare no effort.
We must work this time
and do so much at this moment
that Barrabas is given to us   22,528
and this Jesus hung on a cross.
You, my lords, see to it.
ANNAS My friends, have you heard
the offer that the procurator makes us?   22,532
RUBEN Barrabas must be killed; °
he is a bold thief,
a false and seditious murderer;
and Jesus must be rescued.   22,536
CAIAPHAS Ah, evil people, what do you say?
This Jesus destroys our law;
he wrongs you; he seduces you;
if he is not killed, you will perish.   22,540
ANNAS Come, on evil people, ask for
Barrabas by common agreement!
NEPTALIN This is an incredible idea.
Your talk does not suffice.   22,544
Jesus never did us wrong.
Why do we request his death?
JEROBOAM If there is anyone who insists
on going against our will,   22,548
we will cause him such pain
that he will never get over it.
EMILIUS We will do what pleases you,
my lords, without any restrictions.   22,552
CELSIDON Whom will we request?
MARDOCEE Barrabas.
We want him to be freed.
RABANUS And what about Jesus?
JORAM Delivered to death,
the cruelest death possible.   22,556

22,533 The Pharisees, who are always manipulative in Gréban, confer with the Jews away from Pilate. Ruben and Neptalin exclaim that Jesus has done no wrong. In response, Jeroboam, a Pharisee, threatens them with physical harm if they do not demand Barrabas. Significantly, Gréban has other Jews obey the Pharisees' order while Ruben and Neptalin remain silent, thus expressing their disapproval. When Pilate asks if Barrabas or Christ is to be condemned, they are either again silent or not present (lines 22,613–76). In Marcadé, the Jews spontaneously and uniformly demand Barrabas (lines 14,077–95).

NENBROTH Rest assured that we will ask for him
    as you would wish; I guarantee it.
PILATE Griffon!
GRIFFON My lord.
PILATE Now hurry up
    like a diligent schoolboy.   22,560
    Go and tell the jailer
    that Barrabas is to be unfettered
    and bring him before me
    in chains, right away and immediately;   22,564
    I think that he is in great danger
    of not soon returning.
GRIFFON Ah, he's a choice prey
    for a really hungry gibbet.   22,568
CLAQUEDENT He's a thief with such a bad reputation
    that everyone is displeased with him.
BRAYART Therefore, an old gibbet awaits him
    to make his sepulchre.   22,572
GRIFFON Brayart, to play it safe, come,
    you will help me bring him.
BRAYART Bring or drag,
    it doesn't matter to me which it is.   22,576

                [They go to the prison.]

BRUTAUMONT, *a jailer*
    Where are you going, Griffon? To look at you,
    you seem very busy.
    Your muzzle grimaces
    like the snout of an old hound.   22,580
GRIFFON By the devil, you're on your dung heap.
    That's why you bray so loudly.
    Give me the rascal
    you knocked around last night.   22,584
BRUTAUMONT What rascal are you talking about?
GRIFFON Barrabas.
    You understand no more than a thrush.
BRUTAUMONT {*to Barrabas*}
    Here, here, good sir, don't resist anymore;
    you make such an ugly grimace.   22,588
GRIFFON Come on, buddy, come over here,
    so I can punch you around a little.
    You'll be like the grapes of Vimeu,
    harvested by ladder.   22,592
BARRABAS Alas, what is it?

GRIFFON You'll die a cruel
    death. Do you hear my words?
BRAYART By my faith, that's true.   22,596
    I think there are many better appearances
    than to be covered with your skin.
    I don't ever want such a garment.
BARRABAS I will soon die .
    I hold it certain.   22,600
    I've believed it for a long time
    and greatly deserve it.
    I never loved or served God.
    I never did good in my life,   22,604
    but always lived in hatred,
    envy, and anger.
BRAYART The blazon on your shield
    will be a beautiful crossed gibbet   22,608
    where your body will be broken,
    and where you will die ignominiously.
GRIFFON Here is the worthless scoundrel
    whom I bring before you well bound.   22,612

        [*Pilate places Jesus on his right and Barrabas on his left.*]

PILATE He will not be forgotten. °
    I think he will soon depart
    elsewhere. Now then, my lords,
    here is Barrabas, the deceiver,   22,616
    the false murderer, the robber,
    who has outraged the people.
    On the other side is Jesus,
    who preached to you and instructed you   22,620
    and performed works bearing fruitful results,
    your Christ, your savior.
    Choose, without favoritism,
    which of the two you wish to release   22,624
    for Passover.
EMILIUS It should be made known.
    We seek Barrabas.
CELSIDON We ask you for Barrabas;
    we want him returned to us.   22,628

22,613 The demand for Christ's death, the final condemnation, and the torture of
Christ have their source in Matthew 27:15–31, Mark 15:6–20, Luke 23:17–25, and
John 18:39–19:15.

PILATE And what will I do with Jesus,
    your prophet who is here?
RABANUS Take, take, take him to the gibbet
    and immediately crucify him for us.   22,632
PILATE Your king?
SALMANASAR This word displeases us.
    Take, take, take him to the gibbet!
PILATE Lords, please wait.
    I assure you that I do not see any reason.   22,636
PHARES Take, take, take him to the gibbet
    and immediately crucify him for us.
PILATE What, lords? I trust
    you as men of good counsel,   22,640
    for which reason I am even more surprised
    that you desire that I consent
    to condemning an innocent person
    without knowing how or why.   22,644
    You prize your law so highly,
    defy others so forcefully,
    and justify yourselves so forcefully
    that it seems you value no one.   22,648
    See if your law allows
    you to make such judgments.
    This is not done by a just people.
    Think on it, I beseech you.   22,652
NENBROTH Take him right away and crucify him
    and strike out his name from the earth.
PILATE How dare you request this?
    I think you have gone mad.   22,656
    Will I crucify your king?
    The cross is the most villainous death
    that human nature can suffer.
    Therefore, if he has deserved death,   22,660
    and it is necessary to end his life,
    you can approve a less horrible death
    than hanging on a cross one of such noble blood,
    who boasts of royal blood.   22,664
JEROBOAM Noble governor, never have I called him such.
    This language affronts us too much.
    He is neither our king nor our prince. °
    We deny and disown him,   22,668

22,667–71 John 19:15.

curse and excommunicate him;
we have neither king nor lord
except Caesar, the emperor,
whom alone we wish to obey.   22,672
And you yourself ought to hate him
because he calls himself our king,
thus offending and opposing Caesar,
your master who commissioned you here.   22,676

> [*Pilate enters the praetorium and sits in the
> high seat when delivering Barrabas.*]

PILATE Now I tell you my friends that °
to comply with your desire
and to show that your pleasure
is mine and that I do not want to displease   22,680
you but wish instead to comply completely,
I will give Barrabas to you.
But concerning Jesus, I tell you
that because sentencing him to death   22,684
will cause my conscience remorse,
I would like to defer a little.
I will put him into such a state for you
or I will have my soldiers do so,   22,688
that he will never dare risk
taking the name of king.

> [*Barrabas leaves and Pilate descends from
> the praetorium and comes to the Jews.*]

Guards, prepare yourselves,
you must act in the name of the law.   22,692
GRIFFON It doesn't matter what we have to do; °
we'll do it immediately.

22,677–92 Both Marcadé and Gréban have Pilate delay releasing Barrabas by
proposing a beating. In the former, however, Pilate makes his offer only after his
wife has warned him about the dangers of crucifying Christ.

22,693–962 In Gréban, the torture in these scenes is performed exclusively by the
Romans who are supervised by Pilate. The torturers devise the crown, robe, and
scepter. In Marcadé, the torturers are Jews supervised by Annas and Caiaphas,
who devises the robe and scepter (lines 14,283–722). Pilate is largely absent.
Torments in common include the following: whipping; spitting (limited to a
single stage direction in Gréban; in Marcadé it is a prolonged and disgusting
scene); forcing the crown of thorns onto Christ's head with sticks; pulling Christ's
beard. Marcadé includes blindman's buff, which in Gréban is performed earlier
by the Jews at Caiaphas' court (lines 20,912–50).

[Pilate sits in a chair outside the praetorium while Jesus remains inside.]

PILATE Griffon!

GRIFFON Lord.

PILATE Go tie up
    this Jesus and attach him   22,696
    very tightly to that pole
    with strong rope, at the bottom and top.

GRIFFON Dressed like that?

PILATE What an idiot!
    Don't you hear anything, stupid jerk?   22,700

[The torturers go get him from the praetorium and tie him (to the pillar).]

GRIFFON We must strip him naked.
    I understand your sickness.
    Here, villain, may Jupiter curse you.
    Are you getting worried?   22,704
    Your worthless and despicable body
    will now be reshaped.

ORILLART He has a beautiful and well-formed body;
    it's too bad he's not wise.   22,708

BRAYART His back is well suited
    for receiving many blows.

CLAQUEDENT He'll get ten million of them
    before dinner.   22,712

GRIFFON I agree.
    Now then, pull this bit of rope
    and tie him to this pillar.

CLAQUEDENT If he can untie himself,
    I'll admit that he's very clever.   22,716

GRIFFON Look sir, is this satisfactory?
    Is he tied well on top?

PILATE Very well.

GRIFFON Now then, describe
    what you have in mind.   22,720

PILATE I will tell you in a few words.
    Hop to it, four of you soldiers,
    the biggest and most wicked.
    Make eight or ten beautiful, long,   22,724
    and delightful switches
    and whips braided in cord
    laced with small knots.
    When you have prepared all this,   22,728
    beat him for me in such a way

that there is no place on his whole body
where there is not a wound or a mark.
Can you do this well? 22,732
GRIFFON Until you say "halt"
we will not stop hitting him.
BROYEFORT, *a servant*
While you are skinning him,
I would like to take care of 22,736
making the switches as fast as possible
in order always to have new ones.
Look, here are four beautiful ones;
Let each take one for himself. 22,740
GRIFFON Here's one for me.
CLAQUEDENT And one for me.
I know very well how to use it.
PILATE Griffon, you do nothing but chatter.
Lay on! 22,744
GRIFFON Don't rush.
We must roll up our sleeves
before we can do anything.
PILATE If there's a contemptible thief among you
who hesitates to shake him up, 22,748
no one will be able to prevent
his immediate hanging.
ORILLART He won't wait long.
I'm going to start the fight. 22,752
GRIFFON His skin is already gashed
from the blows I'm giving him.
PILATE Hit, hit hard, you band of scoundrels.
May no man forget what he's doing. 22,756
CLAQUEDENT Do you think I'm missing him, then?
BARRAQUIN Hit, hit hard, you band of scoundrels.
BRAYART We'll tear him piece by piece.
We see nothing but blood on him. 22,760
PILATE Hit, hit hard, you band of scoundrels.
May no man forget what he's doing.
Return him to me so feeble,
so overcome by severe pain, 22,764
that on his body there is not a vein
that is not wounded to death.
ORILLART He'll receive enough of our blows
that it will hardly please him. 22,768
GRIFFON Give me some switches!
BROYEFORT How many?

GRIFFON Two pairs.
    Mine are no good anymore.
CLAQUEDENT Broyefort, you certainly make us squawk.
    Give me some switches!   22,772
BROYEFORT How many?
CLAQUEDENT Two pairs.
BROYEFORT Hey there, so much talk!
ORILLART And so much to do!
    We won't finish this way.
    Give me some switches!
BROYEFORT How many?
ORILLART Two pairs.
    Mine are no good any more.   22,776
BROYEFORT Orillart's really hurting him now;
    it's clear from the way he works.
    He's taken so much blood from him
    that you can't tell his ass from his head.   22,780
ORILLART He's only beginning to join the feast;
    the strongest will be first.
    Give us some switches, Broyefort,
    or you'll be accused of making a mistake.   22,784
BROYEFORT Hey, you devils, you really need a lot!
    What demon would be able to supply you?
BRAYART This is not enough to punish him.
    Switches are only for children.   22,788
    For such a big and powerful scoundrel
    a much more severe deterrent is necessary.
GRIFFON Explain to us what kind,
    so that we may fight him.   22,792
ORILLART Do you recommend
    fists or sticks?
BRAYART Neither; instead, fine whips
    knotted at the ends
    with big, beautiful knots.   22,796
BROYEFORT What are you talking about?
    Here's whatever you ask for.

[Each one takes a whip.]

PILATE Come on boys, you're giving up!
    Recover your breath and strength   22,800
    and return him to me so beaten
    on all sides that there's nothing left to beat.
GRIFFON One.
ORILLART And two.

BRAYART And three.
CLAQUEDENT And four
    and a fifth for good measure.   22,804
GRIFFON A mad man deserves such treatment.
    One.
ORILLART And two
BRAYART And three.
CLAQUEDENT And four.
BROYEFORT Griffon, you count without adjusting,
    for one blow you hit three times.   22,808
GRIFFON When there are ten, make a cross.
    I just do it for fun.
    One.
ORILLART And two
BRAYART And three.
CLAQUEDENT And four.
    And the fifth for good measure,   22,812
    who will give it to him?
GRIFFON If you take my advice,
    strike him a strong blow.
BROYEFORT It seems that Brayart doesn't touch him,
    but by the soul of my good father,   22,816
    he doesn't deliver a stroke without marking
    a wound four fingers wide.

Here they beat him a while without speaking

PILATE Hey, that's enough for this time.
    Men, stop the beating.   22,820
    He's had so much that he can't take it any longer.
    I have had to witness great horror.
    Lords, look at the ghastly way
    this scoundrel has been treated.   22,824
    There's not a heart that wouldn't pity him,
    even if it's harder than steel.
GRIFFON By your command, tell us
    what to do after this.   22,828
PILATE It displeases me to see this;
    he bears such terrible chastisement.
    Go poor man, go get dressed.
    I think your accusers   22,832
    are satisfied with the severe pain
    with which you are bitterly punished.
ORILLART There only remains for him to be banished
    so that there will never be news of him.   22,836

GRIFFON I have a much better plan,
    if my lord grants it.
PILATE What do you want done to him,
    Griffon; tell us your idea.   22,840
GRIFFON Sir, I understand that this wretch
    boasted throughout the country
    that he is lord and king of the Jews.
    It is one of the allegations made against him.   22,844
    Therefore, if you want to please
    the Jews who accuse him of this
    and who deny and refuse to accept it,
    I'll tell you what we we'll do;   22,848
    we'll dress him with the garment of a king,
    the most shameful way we can,
    and then we'll show him to them
    bloodied all over,   22,852
    and he'll be the king of fools
    as a sign of derision.
    Isn't this a good idea?
PILATE Your opinion
    pleases me and seems good to me.   22,856
CLAQUEDENT Here is an appropriate garment.
    with which he will be very richly endowed;
    it is an old royal robe with many holes,
    more torn than an old rag.   22,860

      [*Note that there must be an old garment lined
         with marten and ripped at the edges.*]

BRAYART Now then let's give it to him,
    since my lord consents.
    It is proper.
GRIFFON It's worth anything
    to really mock him.   22,864
    Here, false rascal, come over to me.
    Here's what you'll wear.
    Extend your arms.
CLAQUEDENT Why don't you strike
    as soon as you see him back away?   22,868
BRAYART Now here, here, hypocrite, put on
    this garment. Is it becoming?
ORILLART God, what a king!
GRIFFON God, what a dignitary!
    You can tell a mile off that he's a king.   22,872
CLAQUEDENT We must put the scepter

in his hand or we've done nothing.
BRAYART Here's a well-shaped reed
    for making a scepter that's exactly right.   22,876
ORILLART Now let us seat him here on the side,
    in a state of royalty.

            [They seat him on a low chair.]

GRIFFON May he be laid up with a fever
    for all the trouble he gives us!   22,880
CLAQUEDENT May Jupiter send you misfortune!
    Fool, you're forgetting the best!
    Since he is king and governor,
    mustn't we crown him?   22,884
BROYEFORT I'll go make him a crown
    well-suited to his rank.

            [He goes to prepare the crown.]

BRAYART In the meantime, we'll amuse ourselves
    by hitting him on the head   22,888
    with large reeds.
ORILLART Now rejoice,
    sir king, jack of all trades, master of none. °
GRIFFON Hey, greetings, *rex Judeorum!* °
    Isn't the land of Judea   22,892
    very fortunate and much improved
    by having such a ruler?
CLAQUEDENT, *spitting on his face*
    Fie on the king!
BRAYART Fie on the false liar!
    Is a king made of such an idiot?   ·   22,896
    It's too bad and a pity that we don't burn
    such fools who raise themselves so high.

            [He approaches with the crown.]

BROYEFORT Look, here's what's needed
    to crown him nobly.   22,900
ORILLART Here is a rich crown

22,890 *maistre Aliboron.* Hypothetical name in the Middle Ages for the Arab philosopher, Al-Biruni (Combarieu du Grès and Subrenat, 518). Cohen (*Le livre de conduite,* 333) explains that the name comes from the plant name *elleborum,* "hellebore," which was incorrectly interpreted as the name of a philosopher of antiquity. He offers the translation, "Jack of all trades, master of none."
22,891 *rex Judeorum,* "King of the Jews."

to match his distinguished garments;
There are no sapphires or rubies,
but big, prickly thorns.   22,904
GRIFFON I have here I don't know how many,
which will do him a lot of harm.
Now let's put on his head
the crown, which I think is authentic.   22,908
CLAQUEDENT Oh, the devil.
BRAYART What's the matter?
CLAQUEDENT I've pricked myself.
This is a very bad mistake.
BROYEFORT You really are a simpleton
and a hick and stupid.   22,912
Don't you have any other idea?
The solution is obvious and simple.
ORILLART And that is?
BROYEFORT Take in your hand
very big, heavy, and gnarled sticks   22,916
and strike him forcefully,
so that they gash him or break.
ORILLART That's a good plan.
We'll do it that way.   22,920

[*Using sticks, they force the crown on him.*]

Come on, come on, we must make it fit him
by force, no matter what!
Strike him from there!
GRIFFON To look at him,
he grits his teeth from great torment.   22,924
Here is a noble crown
for a great, worldly prince.
CLAQUEDENT The spoon matches the pot, °
and the sock fits the leg. °   22,928
But the more we strike, the more it pops up.
I don't know what devil's stopping it.
BRAYART He has a devilishly big head;
we are fixing the crown on him with great difficulty.   22,932
ORILLART Look at the thorns pierce him.
Some are exceptional
and these have penetrated into

22,927 *a tel pot tel cuillier.* A proverb (Jodogne, 448).
22,928 *selon la gembe la chausse.* A proverbial phrase (Hassell, 140).

the very center of his brain.   22,936
GRIFFON Long live our new king,
    who now holds a royal court!
CLAQUEDENT He wears a magnificent hat,
    but his garment is a little bit dirty.   22,940
BRAYART Where are his shield bearers
    that they do not come here in great numbers?
ORILLART His great troop of table companions
    thinks he is preaching his sermons.   22,944
    I ask that we decorate him
    with blows to finish this off.
GRIFFON Look at the gushing blood
    that bloodies his muzzle.   22,948
    Hey, false and cursed man,
    I feel no pity for your pain,
    no more than for an old man spouting nonsense,
    who's paid with a gibbet instead of grain.   22,952
CLAQUEDENT Shall we play at plucking his beard?
    It's grown far too long.
BRAYART The most valiant will be
    the one grabbing the biggest fistful.   22,956
ORILLART I've already grasped it so firmly
    that his flesh and bright blood
    came off with it.
GRIFFON Wow, he goes in close
    and mustn't I do the same?   22,960
    I don't know what I was thinking of.
    I want to pay him a little visit.
PILATE Lords, enough of this game.
    It started long enough ago.   22,964
    Bring him here to me
    exactly in the state he's in.
    His martyrdom so disturbs me
    that I can hardly look at him.   22,968

    [Jesus is brought to Pilate who exits the praetorium and,
      holding Jesus by the hand, shows him to the Jews.]

Look here, Jewish nobles,
look here, at this sorrowful man,
see what this man endures,
if anyone ever bore such a weight!   22,972
Consider that he is a man,
a most wretched man.

All beasts love their own kind; °
let, then, the semblance of humanity   22,976
moderate your inhumanity.
He is your brother; you see this.
If you were strongly moved
and felt the hate of anger   22,980
because he wanted to call himself your king,
then look at his pitiful royalty,
the most miserable royalty
existing today or that will ever be.   22,984
He will never again make himself king;
it brings about too bitter a punishment.
Look at the crown he wears,
the cloak, the royal scepter;   22,988
He feels such pain in his body
that he will never make use
of any of his limbs; he is finished.
I am acquitted of my duty,   22,992
I ask that this suffice you,
and that you forgive the rest.
NATHAN He must be hung on a cross
or we will not be at all satisfied.   22,996
PILATE Alas, this is a high price to pay
if he must be hung on a cross,
and the good end for which I strive
is poorly understood.   23,000
NACHOR He must be hung on a cross
or we will not be at all satisfied.
JEROBOAM Procurator, these are just vain contentions
which excuse and justify him.   23,004
You must crucify him
or the people will still clamor.
PILATE Ah noble gods of the great temples °
advise me! Alas, what will I do?   23,008
Here is the most passionate fury
of people ever seen!
Here is rage so surprising
that the more it emerges, the more it spreads.   23,012
Never did a lioness or a leopard

22,975 *Toute beste ayme son semblable.* A proverb (Jodogne, 448).
23,007–26 Marcadé's Pilate focuses exclusively on what will happen to himself if
he does not condemn Christ (lines 14,858–89).

possess such cruelty.
In truth, lords, how
I am shocked by your conduct! 23,016
What more harm can you do
to this poor man? What moves you?
He suffers so much that he can stand no more.
He must not be further wounded, 23,020
he is already half-dead.
His death must not be sought,
he is already dead or nearly so.
He is a poor, severely wounded man, 23,024
all cut up and maimed,
who only awaits death to seize him.
EMILIUS Procurator, make sure he doesn't escape.
You've done nothing if he's not crucified very well 23,028
and put to death.
That is our request.
CAIAPHAS You seek delay for nothing.
You see that the people are agitated 23,032
and that he must die. It must be so.
Rid us of these errors.
PILATE Ah, my lords!
ANNAS What do you mean, "my lords"?
He deserves a harsh death 23,036
and you must make him end his life.
It is the end of such malefactors.
CELSIDON He has done so many evil deeds
that he will die for them. 23,040
PILATE This is through envy.
Ah, my lords!
MARDOCEE What do you mean, "my lords"?
He deserves a harsh death.
RABANUS He has done so much, here and elsewhere,
that the people rise up. 23,044
SALMANASAR Take him away, take him away and crucify him!
Do you want to spare such rabble rousers?
PILATE Ah, my lords!
NAASON What do you mean, "my lords"?
He has deserved a harsh death, 23,048
and you must make him end his life.
It is the end of such malefactors.
ELYACHIM You have heard his accusers
through whom we know his misdeeds. 23,052
Moreover, we have good laws

that our God ordained,
and he gave us through them the judgment
that Jesus must die here and now,   23,056
for he made himself the son of God
and commits many other blasphemies.
PILATE Why do you not take him yourselves
and bring him to be crucified?   23,060
You want me to take the responsibility
and, in short, it's not my duty.
ANNAS You hear the accusation we bring against him.
To be more worthy, he has called himself,   23,064
in many places, the son of God,
which calls for the penalty of death.
PILATE Son of God! Why, that's another matter. °
When you accused him before,   23,068
you did not bring up this point.
He must be examined on it.

Here Pilate enters the praetorium, brings Jesus there, and says

Now come here, speak to me Jesus. °
Answer only on one single point.   23,072
Where are you from? You do not speak at all.
Do you bear such arrogance towards me?
Do you not know that I have the power
to free you immediately   23,076
or destroy you or deliver you to death?
You bear such hatred vainly.
JESUS You would have no power over me
if you had not received it from above.   23,080
Therefore if what you say is wrong,
there is clearly sin in it.
In any case, the one who delivered me to you
has the greater sin.   23,084

Here Pilate approaches the Jews

PILATE Lords, I am astonished
that you do not wish to hear reason,
but deviously strive for
the death of this man.   23,088
He is so chastised

23,067–70 John 19:4.
23,071–84 John 19:10–11; *Passion d'Arras* (lines 14,890–917).

～ 88 ～

that it is painful to look at him.
What more is wanted of him?
His misdeed has not been proved by anything.   23,092
The more I examine him, the less I find him
worthy of being sentenced to death.
For God's sake, let's give him a reprieve.
Or if you do not wish to do this   23,096
take him and go °
judge him by your justice,
for this judgment does not pertain
either to me or my office.   23,100
BANNANIAS Procurator, you commit a great trespass
against the imperial orders
when you perceive public evils
and do not punish them with severity.   23,104
If you let this bold intriguer go, °
you are not a friend of Caesar.
This is easy to prove, for
any man who wishes to call himself king,   23,108
wishes to oppose Caesar's laws,
and you wish to tolerate him.
JOATHAN If you do not offer him up on the cross,
Caesar will not be pleased with you   23,112
and maybe will deprive you
of the post he entrusted to you.
PILATE Here are a people wholly dominated by evil!
Here are a most depraved people!   23,116
Here are the least moderate people
born on earth.
The heart in their bosom afflicts them
when they see this scoundrel live.   23,120
Only on account of envy
are they against him for nothing.
O poor man, it truly displeases me
that I must sentence you to death.   23,124
I was made judge in an inauspicious time,
but I must accede
for fear of paying dearly.
These people will not leave me in peace   23,128
until they have their wish.

23,097 John 18:38.
23,105–6 John 19:12.

O good sirs, hear my voice.
Since I know your feelings
which do not allow you to refrain from   23,132
driving this poor man to death,
I will sit at the tribunal
to judge him as must be done,
even though I sense the evil that will come of it.   23,136
Let whoever wishes to hear the final sentence,
go there.
EMILIUS Ah false, wretched prophet,
this time you will be destroyed!   23,140
CELSIDON Let's follow, let's follow, since it concerns us
  to see the matter concluded.
ADAM, *in Limbo*
O God, who reign without end
and who wish to give every good   23,144
to your favorite creature,
when will you signal the hour
in which you are to heal us,
making reparation for our forfeiture?   23,148
When will the wonderful event come
when your dear son will endure death
to terminate our pain?
The wait is painful and hard   23,152
and lasts such a long time
that we do not know how to end it.
EVE Sovereign and divine essence,
knowing all in your foreknowledge   23,156
and seeing what is necessary for us,
look at our calamity
and painful afterlife
which you allow us to suffer.   23,160
When will that time come,
when through your grace and will
we will see your divine presence?
Alas, when will we take the path   23,164
about which David, in his psalter,
sings in great reverence of you?

Silete °

GOD It is time that the very grave offense
      staining the human race   23,168
      be annulled and its sin
      pardoned and the sinner acquitted
      by the glorious merits
      of the Passion to which my son   23,172
      offers himself; he makes me an offering of it
      as the price of redemption
      and to give great joy
      to the human race which, banished and hidden,   23,176
      awaits him in Limbo.
      Michael, my glorious messenger,
      you will make the journey
      to Limbo, where they languish,   23,180
      and there comfort my friends.
      You will tell them that very soon
      they will be relieved of the suffering
      in which they have dwelled a long time.   23,184
MICHAEL Most sovereign eternity,
      reigning in perfect glory,
      your will shall be done
      without delay.   23,188

Here he goes to Limbo and says

Take comfort,
friends, who have been sent here.
You will soon be freed.
Your mighty redemption,   23,192
very timely and most sufficient,
is ready to make itself known
to God and will bring you to safe harbor.
The most blessed son of God,   23,196
Jesus, the gentle and the gracious,
has given himself of his own free will
into the hands of his adversary
and is humbling himself under his hand   23,200
to deliver you, the human race.
Show yourselves to be loyal servants

23,166 *Silete* indicates the playing of music or singing. It also has the function of quieting the spectators at solemn moments.

                      and thank your creator
                      who comes to give you help.   23,204
ADAM   O one and sovereign protector,
                      to whom alone I turn in need
                      in my guilty distress,
                      I've awaited your mercy for many a day   23,208
                      in this long and oppressive sojourn.
                      Now this news makes me rejoice.
EVE   Noble eternal majesty,
                      giving us this joyous hope   23,212
                      out of your supreme goodness,
                      we render you perpetual glory
                      and thank with grateful hearts
                      the angel who reveals it to us.   23,216
ISAIAH   Let us have feasts and sumptuous entertainment,
                      at the arrival of this news,
                      which has completely comforted
                      the assembly of the doleful.   23,220
EZECHIEL   We have long been wretched,
                      but, like newly strengthened people,
                      let us have feasts and sumptuous entertainment
                      at the arrival of this news.   23,224
JEREMIAH   God, strong and powerful over all others,
                      a noble, revered force,
                      has thrust such joy on us
                      that we consider ourselves most fortunate.   23,228
DAVID   Let us have feasts and sumptuous entertainment
                      at the arrival of this news
                      which has completely comforted
                      the assembly of the doleful.   23,232

                Here some motet can be sung

LUCIFER   Dark and tenebrous devils, °
                      odious and villainous troop,

23,233–492 Lucifer's worry over losing the souls in hell is justified because he
overhears Adam, Eve, and the Prophets rejoicing at their coming deliverance. No
such preparation exists in Marcadé, thus Satan's immediate understanding of the
impending loss upon hearing the Jews demand Christ is awkward. In Gréban,
Satan rejoices at Christ's death until he is corrected by Lucifer. In Marcadé, Satan
warns Pilate's wife of the serious practical consequences of condemning Christ;
in Gréban, he also cautions her on the immorality of the act. In Gréban, as in the
Old French and Latin versions of *The Gospel of Nicodemus*, but not as in Marcadé,
Pilate's wife speaks to her husband through an intermediary (Thiry, 61).

who is it that feels such joy
in our terrible black prison?   23,236
BERICH The human race.
LUCIFER Argh! really?
Is that what I heard?
What devil has made them rejoice so,
and what demon makes them sing?   23,240
CERBERUS I think they're trying to bewitch us
by babbling in our ears.
ASTAROTH It's the devil who wakes them up
and makes them dance around the house.   23,244
FERGALUS Indeed, or a fatal despair
by which they are so tormented
because they feel themselves condemned
in the end to the eternal swamp.   23,248
LUCIFER Don't talk to me about it, Fergalus,
nor you others, you cursed troop!
There is worse that you're not telling me.
I fear having a *quid pro quo*. °   23,252
Argh, devils, argh, argh,
venomous and evil dragons,
don't ever believe me again,
if they do not have the firm hope   23,256
of being soon delivered
and escaping from our prisons.
BERICH Lucifer, we lose nothing
if they can find a ploy,   23,260
for if that should happen,
we will immediately remedy it.
LUCIFER False serpents, we will lose them
and be deprived of them.   23,264
I have always apprehended this,
and so it will happen to us,
and this false Christ will come
to despoil all our heritage.   23,268
ASTAROTH Ah, master, you're telling us extraordinary things!
Such talk does not sit well with us.
Since they are condemned to be here,
how will they leave?   23,272
LUCIFER Devils, you are not clever at all.
Once I had you inquire

23,252 *quid pro quo*. Something given or received for something else.

if Christ, about whom many books are written,
had been born on earth.   23,276
After arguments and disputes,
it was said with certainty
that whoever fasted forty days
was Christ and he would show this   23,280
by performing noble deeds,
surpassing the works of nature.
Now I do not know if by chance
he is dead or martyred   23,284
and rapidly coming to
liberate all our prisoners.
FERGALUS I don't fear him a bit,
if he is the one described before.   23,288
LUCIFER He calls himself Jesus,
a holy and virtuous man.
There's hardly a devil in our hell
who does not recognize him   23,292
and to whom he has not caused so much anguish
that it cannot be told or measured.
BERICH I know him well by reputation.
He is a man of great stature.   23,296
But if he comes, he will nonetheless
encounter a strong and terrible battle.
CERBERUS If he comes here to pillage our suburbs,
I, in play and mockery,   23,300
will keep my door shut
in order to resist him.
LUCIFER Cerberus, you must be on guard.
You'll be hanged if you don't run off.   23,304
SATAN Hooray, how happy I am!
Hooray! I've obtained such joy,
nourished by fiery rage
in having worked so well.   23,308
I've won everything; I've won everything.
I've done a great deed, a masterpiece.
My heart takes such delight
when I plan well and with precision.   23,312
Jesus is dead; he's done for.
Pilate is going to sentence him!
It's no longer necessary to stay here.
I'm immediately going to hell,   23,316
half howling, half singing,
for when Lucifer learns this,

I know he'll feel such elation
that I'll be crowned there, 23,320
for never did any damned fiend
do better work.
Lucifer, you horrible stork,
ceaselessly brooding over the nest of pride, 23,324
devils, dearer than father and mother,
arouse yourselves and gather round.
LUCIFER How are you Satan, good brother?
Will you tell us some miracle? 23,328
SATAN I have committed a murder greater
than any devil in hell ever could.
LUCIFER How?
SATAN Jesus, our adversary,
is taken, bound, and chained 23,332
and is about to be crushed,
if the devil doesn't stick his paw into it.
At this time he is with Pilate
who will condemn him to death. 23,336
LUCIFER What the devil are you saying?
SATAN My report
is true just as I'm telling you.
LUCIFER Ah false devil, full of disgrace,
do you tell us this? 23,340
False Satan, you have ruined everything!
False fiend, horrible and black,
you have destroyed our manor,
if you do not find the means 23,344
to ensure that nothing comes of this deed.
This Jesus will destroy us.
This Jesus will strip us.
It is for him that all these prophets 23,348
have now felt such joy.
It is for him that they play and sing.
It is because of him that they boast so loudly
of soon escaping despite us. 23,352
They think they'll be rescued by him.
News of it has come to them.
Vile and corrupt substance,
rabid dog, more stinking than a dunghill, 23,356
quickly go back where you've come from
and find the means to undo
what you wanted to do
or you will pay for it horribly. 23,360

You will go to Pilate's wife
who still sleeps in her bed
and show her, through a great miracle,
that all those who are involved in   23,364
and make themselves guilty
of the death of Jesus, the preacher,
will be condemned.

SATAN Be assured
that I'll make this my first duty.   23,368

LUCIFER Now go, running and shouting!
May you be guided and led
by the whole abyss of the damned!

Here Satan goes to Pilate's wife, who must be in her bed

SATAN I didn't take too long   23,372
in coming to this place.
It's the city of Jerusalem.
So now I must
find the means, through trickery,   23,376
to have Jesus escape
or else I'll be destroyed.
Lucifer instructed me well on this,
so I cannot fail to follow my orders.   23,380
O man, sleeping right here,
behold now a dream
in which there is no illusion.
Listen to what I recount to you.   23,384
Your husband holds a very holy and innocent
man who never did wrong;
he is Jesus, who calls himself Christ,
and because of the envy people bear him,   23,388
they want to condemn him to death,
over which your husband wishes to be judge.
Make sure that he does not judge him,
for if he gives the death sentence,   23,392
it is against right and conscience.
Afterwards, you will see a time
when you and he will be destroyed
and will undergo punishment   23,396
for the wrongful execution
which he will order. Remember this well.
Make sure that it never happens to him.
Prevent this as much as you can   23,400
or you will die horribly

and soon, I guarantee you.

PILATE'S WIFE O Venus, in whom I have faith,
Pallas, Jupiter, and Mercury,   23,404
what a sad and dark vision
I saw last night during my sleep!
I commend myself to you, my gods.
I have great need of your help,   23,408
for my heart trembles in terror
of what you have revealed to me.
I see many people assembled there,
making great noise and great cries.   23,412
Sardina, what's this? I beg you
tell me what it is, so I will know.

SARDINA *the chambermaid*
My lady, I will tell you
as I understand it.   23,416
Those are Jews, who had Jesus,
the good and saintly man, arrested,
and with a will full of venom
arising from envy of him   23,420
they besiege your husband,
demanding to have him crucified
without delay,
for which some are very happy   23,424
and others so sorrowful
that it is pitiful to hear them.

PILATE'S WIFE O Sardina, you must run
to my husband without any delay   23,428
and tell him to refrain,
before doing anything wrong,
from making this man suffer,
even though the people cry out to him.   23,432
Tell him that I beg him
to save this man from their hands if he can,
and that this very night
I had a brief vision of him   23,436
so overwhelming and so distressing
that my heart still trembles from it.
The vision plainly showed me
that whoever is guilty   23,440
of his unfortunate and miserable death
will end his days in pain.

SARDINA My lady, without waiting any further,
I will not fail you in any of it.   23,444

PILATE'S WIFE Commend me to him,
    and may he carefully consider his action.
SARDINA Do not fear anymore; it will be done
    completely according to your will.   23,448

Here she approaches Pilate

PILATE I am now seated in majesty
    on the seat of high justice,
    as is proper to my rank,   23,452
    to judge fairly.
    Nevertheless, lords, I feel terrible about
    the predicament of this poor man
    on whom you do not wish to have mercy,
    despite all the beating and torment he has received.   23,456
    Can't you restrain
    the ardor which inflames your hearts,
    if you do not see his soul
    leave his body without some reprieve?   23,460
SARDINA My lord, would it displease you
    if I say a couple of words to you,
    away from the others?
PILATE On what subject?
    Say them quickly, I command you.   23,464
SARDINA My lady commends herself to you
    sir, and begs you in her distress that,
    for the sake of the pleasure and love
    which you always give her,   23,470
    this man whom you hold
    may be rescued from death
    and, no matter what happens, that you
    not sentence him yourself, if he must die.   23,472
PILATE I want neither to help nor to harm him.
    I am not myself involved.
    But I beg you by your faith,
    what moved her to send this message?   23,476
SARDINA She saw last night, while sleeping,
    great marvels of high portent
    concerning this Jesus, as she recounts,
    which she will tell you later.   23,480
    But whatever happens, she told me expressly
    that you should rid yourself of this matter
    and should take care not to judge him,
    no matter what pretext they give you.   23,484
PILATE Don't worry. All will be well,

if I can manage it in any way.
Go then and assure her
that, at her request,   23,488
I will do my utmost
for his deliverance.
SARDINA My lord,
may our gods grant that you conduct yourself
honorably!   23,492

Here she returns to her mistress

PILATE Again, I would like to find out
if this contentious people
will ever be appeased
or if they may wish to retract.   23,496

[*He must step down from the high seat and go to the Jews.*]

Now good lords, I ask you
in love and true friendship
that you look with pity
on your king and restrain yourselves   23,500
and consider a little
his unfortunate rule.
EMILIUS Take him away and crucify him.
It's painful to look at him.   23,504
JEROBOAM You gain nothing by delaying.
Governor, you play deaf for nothing;
the more you procrastinate, the louder the clamor,
the more you defer, the more the people   23,508
will exert themselves in crying out.
MARDOCEE It is necessary
that he die; one cannot save him.
If you do not have him die,
you are wasting your time on this matter.   23,512
PILATE Ah people, you do not consider at all
the difficulties a judge takes on
when sentencing a just man to death.
Such a death must be carefully assessed   23,516
and weighed on a scale.
The death of a man is an important matter.
CAIAPHAS Are you offering us this as a conclusion?
Will we stay here all day?   23,520

In short, you are not a real friend °
nor very devoted to Caesar,
if you do not have such a bestial man
die a bitter death.   23,524
He made himself king, that is clear;
and whoever professes himself king
wounds the majesty of Caesar.
You know it better than anyone else.   23,528
Why do you delay
in condemning him to a cursed death?
PILATE Here is a terrible situation.
All my actions are defeated!   23,532
I struggled for nothing
to devise his deliverance.
I so fear offending Caesar
that I do not dare disobey.   23,536
It is necessary that I assail him
and condemn him, whether right or wrong;
otherwise, great harm will come to me hereafter.
I see that this is certainly so.   23,540

[*He must enter the praetorium and sit in the high seat.*]

Now my friends, since it pleases you,
and to be in your good favor,
I must pronounce judgment;
but first, I would like to wash my hands   23,544
according to the custom of the Romans,
who devised this ritual
as a sign of purification.
I can certainly wash my hands of this,   23,548
for I am not the author of his death,
I neither consent to nor support anything.
Barraquin!
BARRAQUIN Revered sir,
what is your wish?   23,552
PILATE Put some water in the washbowl;
prepare a basin and towel,
and when this is done, give them to me.
I am in a great hurry; serve me quickly.   23,556
ARRAQUIN Here it is all ready, sir governor.
Now wash in good health.

23,521–27 A repetition of lines 23,105–6; John 19:12.

PILATE Lords, I exculpate myself °
    and my conscience feels cleared of   23,560
    the death of this innocent and
    just man whom you destroy.
    Therefore, consider what you do.
    You see that I acquit myself of   23,564
    all his blood and charge you with it.
    I hold myself innocent and pure.
EMILIUS Let all his blood flow and descend °
    on all of us and our children,   23,568
    so that they will never be innocent
    if sin or blame is established here.
PILATE You see how I purify myself
    of these very weighty matters.   23,572
RABANUS Let all his blood flow and descend
    on all of us and our children!
    Do you fear him so much?
PILATE More than anyone else in the world.
SALMANASAR Why?   23,576
PILATE The dangers are great,
    for you show yourselves too desirous
    of finding tricks to destroy him.
NEMBROTH Let all his blood flow and descend
    on all of us and our children,   23,580
    so that we will never be innocent
    if sin or blame is established here.
PILATE Finally I will make
    my rock and my foundation with this pledge.   23,584
    You truly bind yourselves
    with your public response,
    and I would like to rest
    my judgment on it, briefly and quickly   23,588
    at this time. °

23,559–66 Matthew 27:24; *Passion d'Arras* (lines 15,160–66). Gréban, unlike Marcadé, follows biblical order and has Pilate wash his hands before pronouncing Christ's death sentence.

23,567–68 Matthew 27:25; *Passion d'Arras* (lines 15,167–68). Gréban faithfully translates the biblical passage, while Marcadé has his character add that the Jews are *glad* to have the blood of Christ upon them.

23,589–98 *Passion d'Arras* (lines 15,130–41). Note the legal formality of Pilate's pronouncement. In Marcadé, Pilate sentences both Christ and the thieves without formality and without interruption. In Gréban (23,601–12), Pilate condemns them separately and with less ceremony.

I, Pontius Pilate,
holder, according to well-established charter,
of the governorship of Judea,
placed in this region under Caesar, 23,592
having heard the accusation
against Jesus in his presence,
condemn him and sentence him
to be hanged and left on the cross, 23,596
never to leave it
until his life has ended.
NATHAN Now that the affair is concluded,
my heart feels great joy. 23,600
PILATE Listen to what I say.
Jewish lords, according to your wish
and to my extraordinary sorrow
I have condemned this innocent man. 23,604
Since everyone agrees to it,
I cannot and must not resist.
However, in order to try
several cases all together, 23,608
I still have two evildoers,
evil rogues and thieves.
Decide if we will let them go
or if they will go to the tribunal. 23,612
ANNAS Dear sir, we must try them
before the next festival.
PILATE Griffon, go then, bring them here.
Do you know who they are? 23,616
GRIFFON Certainly.
I would like to be the hangman
to string them up immediately.

Here he goes to the jailor and says:

Open the prison door, Brutaumont,
and hand over those two pilgrims 23,620
who set up ambushes on the roads
and robbed many a good merchant.
I think they'll be going to
the gibbet, since I'm undertaking this. 23,624
BRUTAUMONT The door is open, so you can take them
and pull them out one by one.
GRIFFON Ah, Tervagant, it's so dark in here!
It's as deep as hell. 23,628
BRUTAUMONT They are chained with strong chains

and are very strongly secured.

GRIFFON Boldly grab them by the feet.
    I certainly think it necessary.   23,632

BRUTAUMONT Why?

GRIFFON Because we will hang them
    through the base of their brains.
    Come on, come forth, thief;
    you'll soon be disposed of.   23,636

DYMAS *the good thief*
    May God forgive us all our sins;
    we have committed a great number!

GRIFFON Now you're an honest man!
    but it's only when you can't be anything else.   23,640

GESTAS *the bad thief*
    What then, are our days ended?
    Is there no escape from our end?

DYMAS Brother, I see none.
    There's nothing to do but commend ourselves   23,644
    to God; may he keep for us
    our place in his lofty realm.

GRIFFON Yes, yes, tell it to Guillaume. °
    You'll go to reign somewhere else.   23,648
    Governor, here are the two plunderers;
    think about attending to their business.

PILATE Their trial is already all but done.
    We sentence them to hang on the cross   23,652
    until they give up their souls
    and their lives end there
    in bitter death.

ORILLART What medicine
    to comfort a patient!   23,656

GESTAS Then it's certain.
    We must suffer through this torment.

GRIFFON My lords, you do not mention
    the crosses in your conversations;   23,660
    there must be one for each.
    Decide where we should get them.

PILATE You are right. We will think about it.
    Lords, let us consider   23,664
    by what means you intend

23,647 *c'est a Guillaume*. A number of first names in French have a pejorative sense
(Hassell, 131, citing Doutrepont, 14–16).

to have the scoundrels whom you see before you
crucified as soon as possible.
Do you want the crosses to be all of one kind   23,668
as custom dictates
and as was done in past times?
I tell you this for a particular reason,
because we must speak precisely,   23,672
in accordance with the kind of crucifixion,
so that the crosses be built accordingly.
CAIAPHAS The crosses made
for finishing the two thieves   23,676
can certainly be of one kind,
according to the customary size;
But the one designated for
Jesus, that wicked scoundrel,   23,680
we want it another way
in order to cause him greater dishonor.
PILATE How?
CAIAPHAS We want it larger,
heavier, and also thicker.   23,684
In order to put him in a different category
and for greater torment,
he will be placed differently from the others.
He will be pierced through his feet and hands   23,688
and tightly affixed
to the cross of great height
to die in greater distress,
suffering, pain, and confusion.   23,692
PILATE Are you of this opinion?
It is not customary to see this.
JEROBOAM We want to have it so in order to further
ruin his great reputation.   23,696
PILATE Then I do not want to oppose it;
I will have it done right away.
Griffon, go to my carpenter
and have him construct three crosses   23,700
to display three evildoers.
If he hasn't any that are ready made,
two shall be average sized
and the third, much larger.   23,704
GRIFFON I understand better than you think;
all shall be quickly prepared.
PILATE Broyefort, go the other way
to the blacksmith, to his forge.   23,708

Tell him to forge immediately
three big, long, sharp nails.
BROYEFORT Since it's done to nail Jesus,
    I'd sooner not eat   23,712
    than not have them forged,
    for he's deserved this for some time.
GRIFFON Carpenter, my friend, come here.
    Do you have any crosses?   23,716
CARPENTER How many do you need?
GRIFFON I need three
    for three treacherous scoundrels,
    whom I will lead to the gibbet
    as infamous and dishonest men.
CARPENTER Here are two already prepared;
    they're so heavy that it's horrible.
GRIFFON They're of a good size.
    They're exactly what I need.   23,724
    But I need a taller one
    for another lunatic who's there.
CARPENTER I don't have any wood ready, °
    that has such a large trunk or tall branches,   23,728
    except for an ancient plank
    that has been near this house
    since the time of king Solomon
    and is very beautiful and marvelous.   23,732
GRIFFON Take it then and fix it up.
    It must be made, whatever condition it's in,
    for if my lord becomes angry,
    your situation will certainly end badly.   23,736
CARPENTER I'll immediately do
    my job; I'll go to work right now.
    It seems that my heart moves me
    with joy when I make money.   23,740
GRIFFON It's the custom of such people.
    You think only about money.
BROYEFORT Blacksmith, may the sun and the moon
    watch over you, along with Vulcan!   23,744
    New cases have come upon us,
    rather urgent, as it happens,

23,727–32 The carpenter alludes to but does not tell the story of the origin of the
cross. The full account is given in the *Passion d'Arras* (lines 15,397–449) and in *The
Golden Legend* under the entry for May 3.

for which you absolutely must
work for us right away.   23,748
BLACKSMITH Doing what?
BROYEFORT Forging three nails
with which our procurator plans
to do a great deed.
BLACKSMITH Nothing else?
And you made such a big deal about it. °   23,752
If I may ask, what kinds of nails do you need?
Door nails or window nails
or to shoe a horse expertly?
Tell me quickly to get it done.   23,756
BROYEFORT No, they're for crucifying
an extremely villainous scoundrel
who was seized in this town,
for nailing his feet and hands to the cross.   23,760
BLACKSMITH Is it Jesus?
BROYEFORT None other.
He must die for his excesses.
BLACKSMITH There's not much harm
as long as there was a fair investigation.   23,764
BROYEFORT Forge, forge, and don't chatter any more.
You're all gossip and foolishness.

Here he forges the nails

CARPENTER Here are three well-made crosses,
if ever a man made them well.   23,768
GRIFFON Whoever assigned them their name
showed himself to be ingenious and judicious,
for it is the most terrible torment
possible in this world.   23,772
CARPENTER Do you want to preach to us now?
By the devil, here's a real idiot!
Make sure you have a cart
to take them right away.   23,776
GRIFFON Here is what we'll use.
CARPENTER Now let's load it up
immediately, with little disturbance.
GRIFFON Ah, Jupiter, how heavy this one is!

23,752 In dramatizing the blacksmith's forging of the nails, Gréban omits the
apocryphal legend of the blacksmith's wife, often found in mysteries and included in the *Passion d'Arras*.

I haven't seen one like it in a long time. 23,780
CARPENTER It's big and massive,
    tall and wide from end to end.
GRIFFON That's enough. I'm leaving
    since I've taken my supplies. 23,784

He takes away the three crosses in a cart

BLACKSMITH Here are nails with good sharp points,
    sharp enough to pierce grey marble.
    If they are not excellently forged,
    I ask nothing, good sir. 23,788
BROYEFORT Still I have a bit more to say about
    what displeases and bothers me.
BLACKSMITH What?
BROYEFORT The points are too sharp.
    Make them a little more rounded, 23,792
    so that this evil Jesus
    feels more pain and torment
    when they enter him
    and pierce limb after limb. 23,796
BLACKSMITH You never think of anything
    other than bloody maliciousness.
    Now here, are they well-fashioned?
    What do you think? 23,800
BROYEFORT They're just what I want.
BLACKSMITH And the money?
BROYEFORT You don't need any.
    I don't have any. Let me go.
    My lord will speak to you
    and will remunerate you. 23,804
BLACKSMITH It will never have to be paid,
    since I am thus rewarded.
PILATE It is time to order
    the death of these wrongdoers. 23,808
    All is ready. Therefore, my lords,
    have them brought in again
    and think about the way
    you want them to be arranged. 23,812
ANNAS We want Jesus put
    in the middle of the group,
    so that his great villainy
    be set off by two thieves; 23,816
    in this way we will lead
    all three together to be destroyed

on the mountain of Calvary,
a propitious place for such people.   23,820
CAIAPHAS If we are to be very careful °
about making him more easily recognizable
by those who took him to be holy,
then let us remove this king's garment   23,824
and dress him in the array
in which he usually travelled the roads,
so that each may see him
in his customary clothing.   23,828
JEROBOAM My lord, you have decided well.
We must have him in his own clothes,
so that each may see him
and recognize him more easily.   23,832
PILATE Come on soldiers, hurry up.
Strip this unfortunate one
or I will have no peace from them.
I clearly see that this concerns them.   23,836
GRIFFON My lord, it will be done for you.
Do not worry about it any more.
Orillart, you pull from that side.
You really are a lazy rascal!   23,840

[*They begin to strip Jesus.*]

ORILLART Must he wear only his under tunic?
He has indeed fallen on bad times.
GRIFFON He must be stripped naked.
The rulers want it so.   23,844
CLAQUEDENT Sir, may the devil laugh, but
won't we get to the end of it today?
GRIFFON Now, friend, pull, pull there!
Claquedent, you're useless.   23,848
CLAQUEDENT I can't.
GRIFFON Why?
BRAYART He's right.
His robe holds firmly together
and sticks to his back so tightly
that it must be torn off by force.   23,852
ORILLART It's like flaying a sheep,
the skin comes off with the garment.
CLAQUEDENT He receives so much new torment.

23,821–28 From Nicholas of Lyra (Roy, 230).

His wounds have come back to mind.   23,856

[They strip him naked.]

GRIFFON His robes have been stripped.
    Sir, command us further.
PILATE Take his old clothes
    and put them on him right away.   23,860
GRIFFON I assure you, it shall be done
    as you command.

[They dress him in the seamless robe.]

PILATE Now walk forward.
ORILLART Wait,
    let him be tied well and tightly.   23,864
    If people don't recognize his evil misdeeds,
    he could deceive the crowd.

[They bind his body and arms.]

BRAYART May I be shaved bald if he escapes.
    But consider what a teacher,   23,868
    what a worthy preacher,
    what an excellent king we have.
MARDOCEE *Ave*, then, *rex Judeorum.* °
    Jewish citizens, come here   23,872
    and bow humbly
    before this king full of virtue.

Here they bow before him.

NAASON *Ave rex!*
ELYACHIM *Et ave Cristus!*
    Noble king of the Jews, may God protect you.   23,876
GRIFFON Say *ave* master idiot!
    That name suits him twice as well.
PILATE Lords, he is mocked enough
    and so well that, to tell the whole truth,   23,880
    there is nothing left to ridicule.
    He is dealt such pain
    that no mortal creature
    does not feel horror in looking at him.   23,884
    It's no longer fitting to rail at him.
    I beg you, lead him out to die

23,871 *Ave, donc, rex Judeorum.* "Hail, then, King of the Jews."

and you'll be doing a charitable act.
If you do not hurry his death,   23,888
you will see him pass away
and die here at this moment.
ANNAS Procurator, each one of us agrees
that he should be quickly led away,   23,892
but we have decided
that he should walk to the location
exactly in between the two thieves.
Furthermore, to inflict more severe pain   23,896
we have ordered that he carry
his cross himself, without any help.
PILATE By all my gods, I am really horrified
by the harshness with which you treat him   23,900
as a harsh people; you are such that
you have absolutely no pity.
But I will not contradict you at all.
I am satisfied, all things considered.   23,904
Go put the murderer to death.
I do not plan to prevent it.
GRIFFON Here, Jesus, you must undertake
to carry this beautiful burden.   23,908
CLAQUEDENT He'll carry it very well,
and if he doesn't shoulder it quickly,
I'll give him such a great blow
that I'll break his spine.   23,912
PILATE Trumpeter, blow the trumpet
very loudly, with a clamorous sound,
so that those of the region,
all officers together,   23,916
mount immediately on horseback
to come to the place of execution.
PILATE'S TRUMPETER I won't be lazy about that.
I'll blow so loudly   23,920
that, by blowing, I'll astound
all those who are in the city.

Here he blows the trumpet.

CENTURION My people, it is necessary
for us to go to the assembly   23,924
that I hear has been called
to carry out the death of Jesus.
RUBION *Centurion's first man of arms*
The Jews had him watched so much

that they seized him for their advantage, 23,928
and now they're taking him in great dishonor
to be disgracefully crucified.
ASCANIUS *second man of arms* Let us follow quickly.
We must appear there, 23,932
for fear that we'll be made to pay
by the emperor's procurator.
CENTURION Look, what great horror!
How he's put to pitiable torment, 23,936
when they make him carry his cross
over such an agonizing path!
RUBION They caught him in some theft,
for they're leading him between two thieves. 23,940
ASCANIUS Then they do well in making the effort to
carry out his death without delay.

Here they go to mount Calvary

GRIFFON My heart feels great anger
because this hypocritical old dog 23,944
doesn't step lightly.
He's as lazy as the devil.
ORILLART Walk, detestable old rogue!
Carry your gibbet forward! 23,948
BRAYART He acts too much like a beggar.
Come on, go ahead, scoundrel, walk fast!
CLAQUEDENT Pull in front there, Broyefort!
Make him climb that path. 23,952
Pull hard!
BROYEFORT And you push from behind!
You do nothing but gab.
JULIA *first woman* O women, come look at °
the great shame! Step forth! 23,956
Jesus, the holy and kindly prophet
who used to do us so much good,
and who was so essential
in helping the poor people, 23,960
goes to die pitifully
through a terrible execution.
VERONICA *second woman* I feel such great compassion,

23,955–24,061 Luke 23:27–31 mentions a multitude of people and women. This
scene occurs in Marcadé after Simon the Leper takes up the cross (lines 15,972–
16,034).

Julia, my dear friend,   23,964
that I receive no comfort today
because I have such great pity in my heart.
PERUSINA *third woman* Alas, Veronica, dear sister,
    alas, who will comfort us?   23,968
    Alas, who will show us
    the holy, divine word?
    Ah, most treacherous intrigue,
    traitorous and cursed Jews,   23,972
    will you kill such a worthy man,
    will your hearts be so brazen?
    O truly sweet God of paradise
    I ask that, in your clemency,   23,976
    you may grant my prayer today
    and give patience to your son.
PASITHEA *fourth woman* ° In tears and in lamentation
    I lament for you Jesus,   23,980
    holy and good man,
    and make my complaints
    because I see these people full of
    hidden venom.   23,984
JULIA Holy and divine man,
    adept at and fond of
    comforting us,
    you go to your end   23,988
    in order to
    support us.
VERONICA Alas, sweet Jesus,
    nobly adorned   23,992
    with all virtues,
    what happened to
    the dearly cherished deeds,
    the good order   23,996
    which you gave to
    your good friends?
    You are badly rewarded
    in being led so   24,000
    and subjected to death.
PERUSINA Jesus, true preacher, °

23,979 The next twenty-two lines have only five syllables each.
24,002–14 A fatras (Porter, 164). A fatras is a verse form consisting of an opening
distich followed by eleven lines, the last of which repeats the second half of the

we will weep for you.
Jesus, true preacher,   24,004
and most solemn teacher,
we will remain without you.
You used to be a guide
and leader of the people;   24,008
now we will lose you.
Alas, what will we do, we who
have no one to console us?
We will be lost,   24,012
and for this, true pastor,
we will weep for you.
PASITHEA We will live in discontentment
under the sway of sadness,   24,016
deprived of joy
at this piteous departure.
JULIA Lament very piteously,
Jerusalem, laudable city.   24,020
Bemoan the pitiable destiny
which falls upon you on this piteous day.
Grieve and weep without cease
mournful, unfortunate city.   24,024
If you are sad and lachrymose,
you have good reason for this suffering,
for you lose the good and the love
by which you should have been glorified.   24,028
VERONICA O noble, honored person,
the most holy under the heavens,
great wrong is done to you and, may God help me,
everyone sees it; each one judges it.   24,032
Cursed be the traitorous judge
when he passed judgment
and when he pronounced the sentence
without offering just reasons.   24,036
JESUS Daughters born of Jerusalem, °
ladies of great devotion,
cease your lamentations,
which so pain your heart.   24,040
Please weep for me no longer

---

distich. According to Porter, Gréban seems to have been the first to include this
form in a *mystère*.
24,037–60 Luke 23:28–31

nor lament, devout women,
but weep for yourselves
and also for your children,   24,044
for the days will soon come
when they will say in a sad voice,
"Blessed by God are the barren wombs
that never bore a child   24.048
and the breasts that never gave suck."
Then in the anguish of anger
together they will say,
"High mountains, hurry   24,052
and fall upon us,"
and to the low hills, "Now open up
and cover us with earth."
For if in me, who am a green tree,   24,056
such a fiery torment is uncovered
and overwhelms me in its pursuit,
what will happen
to those who are dry trees
and void of fertile sap?   24,060

GRIFFON By your devil
march forward, stinking villain!
Are you going to accuse us here?
You have many tricks   24,064
and will be more clever than Argus
if you escape from this feast.

CAIAPHAS Hit him hard on the arms and head
if he doesn't walk quickly.   24,068

OUR LADY O my son, my only thought,
my only good, my only benefit
and the only delight
I have ever seen,   24,072
where are you now, on what path?
Who transported you far away?
Whoever finds this out
may send me the sad news.   24,076
O my son, where will your dear mother
find you,
search for you,
hold and embrace you?   24,080
Your mother feels immense sorrow for you
and wears the most mournful,
the most distressing, and the most painful expression,
beyond that   24,084

ever borne by any creature.
My son, my sweet image,
and my most holy nursling,
have I lost you?   24,088
MAGDALENE My sweet master, my sweet Jesus,
in what port have you arrived?
Alas what has happened to you?
Dolorous heart,   24,092
sad, pensive, and mournful,
suffocated by cruel sighs,
filled with unsavory tears,
what must you do?   24,096
You lose your master whose occupation
was to make and perfect you.
Now you lose him without doing him wrong;
death presses upon him.   24,100
What sorrow, what pain, what sadness,
what great measure of distress
weigh down my heart with such oppression
that it can no longer hold out!   24,104
O felonious Jews, what moves you
to kill the one who promotes you to
all good and wants only good for you?
Calumny   24,108
is always your condition;
At first, you serve with adulation,
but you sting like a scorpion
when no one is present.   24,112
O Jesus, full of knowledge,
sovereign treasurer of clemency,
who gave me
indulgence for my sins,   24,116
have you withdrawn from me
and were you born to be exposed to danger?
May God, whose obedient son you are,
come to your aid.   24,120

[*Note that Gabriel is still with Mary.*] °

JOSEPH OF ARIMATHEA Dear ladies, in my opinion,
if you do not hurry,
you will never arrive on time

24,120 At line 21,246, Gabriel promised Mary to be her guardian.

before Jesus is put to death.   24,124
I and several of his friends
certainly have already seen him pass,
burdened with a great and high cross,
which makes him suffer piteously,   24,128
and surrounded by a prodigious crowd
taking him to be crucified.
OUR LADY Sweet God, to whom I owe all trust, °
comfort me with your mercy!   24,132
Sweet God, what news is this?
Shall I go or shall I stay?
I am sure that I will die
if I go see the Passion   24,136
and the horrible execution
that befalls my dear child.
Staying here suits me better,
although because of it I might continue to live,   24,140
for my soul strives with my body
and death does not want to separate them.
Stay? How shall I stay?
Will my son give himself to death   24,144
without my trying
to follow and help him
and comfort him until death?
Comfort? Alas, I would not do that,   24,148
but rather would discomfort him
a thousand times over; for when he sees me,
his heart will break with sorrow,
and it will kill the sad mother.   24,152
Alas, since he must give himself to death,
may it please God, my father,
that he take us both together
without separating us.   24,156
I will go. It is my intention.
My son, I bore you faithful company
your whole life.
I would do a great wrong   24,160
to leave you to your death now;
there would be no valid excuse for it.
MARY JACOBI Alas, sister, stay, for God's sake!
The pain will cleave your heart.   24,164

24,131–62 A complaint by the Virgin (Sinclair, 108).

Since it must be so, it is better to have
one afflicted than two destroyed.
We will go, my sister and my son.
We will report on the matter.   24,168
OUR LADY My sweet sister, I am against it.
Not for anything do I want to be absent,
but, if it pleases God, I will be present
through everything that will happen.   24,172
God, if it pleases him, will comfort
the hearts wounded with sorrow.
JOSEPH OF ARIMATHEA Lady, if you would like to come,
we must take the trouble   24,176
to go through this back street
to overtake them,
for you will never be able to pass
through this large street where they are going   24,180
because of the crowd there.
Follow me and I will lead you.
OUR LADY Joseph, I will gladly do it.
May God in his grace lead us there!   24,184
ORILLART This rascal here makes us walk
too slowly in my opinion.
BRAYART Then we must give him some whacks
with a stick across his sides,   24,188
for I have never seen anyone lazier.
CLAQUEDENT Then we must give him some whacks.
ANNAS Soldiers, if you don't hit him,
he will go as he likes.   24,192
GRIFFON Then we must give him some whacks
with a stick across his sides.
PILATE Speed up and make him hurry.
You already see that it's high time.   24,196
If you don't, I assure you,
you'll receive a thrashing.
GRIFFON How the devil will we rush him?
He's carrying such a heavy load   24,200
that he can hardly move forward;
he's completely bent under the burden.
VERONICA O most perfect of the perfect, °

24,203–28 The story of St. Veronica and Christ's imprint on her kerchief is first
dramatized in France in the *Mystère de la Passion Nostre Seigneur* (Runnalls, 56). In
the *Passion d'Arras*, Christ asks her for the cloth so he can wipe off his sweat

O most true Christ, son of God,   24,204
you never harmed any man
and now you suffer such severe pain,
and your gentle body endures so much
that today there is not a more pitiful sight!   24,208
I ask God to protect you
and give you much patience,
just as all your life you have wanted
to remain in perfect innocence.   24,212
Alas, your situation is truly lamentable
when all your body
drips with great drops of sweat!
It must feel great agony!   24,216
With this kerchief, I would like
to wipe your precious face
that was once so gracious
and is now so pale.   24,220

Pause

The imprint of the holy and
precious visage remains with me now;
I consider myself highly honored
in receiving such a worthy gift.   24,224
I will be anxious
to preserve it with all my strength
because of the sweet gracious model
preserved in this image.   24,228
SIMON OF CYRENE It is high time that I set forth
and that I go do my work
in Jerusalem to take care
of my business affairs.   24,232
It's really necessary
that I go right now.
I see many people coming here,
but I don't know what they intend.   24,236
In any case, I won't turn back.
I'll pass right through them,
for I believe none of them
will do me harm.   24,240

(lines 15,869–84).

[*Our Lady and the others arrive near Jesus.*]

SAINT JOHN My mistress, please come look at
    your dear child.
    Look at the state he is in,
    how his face is deformed!   24,244
OUR LADY O my son!

Here Our Lady falls in a faint

MARY JACOBI She has fainted.
    Her heart fails, the blood drains from her face!
    As a result, if death follows,
    dear sister, we lose everything!   24,248
MARY CLEOPHAS Sister, in the name of God, let us lift her
    and by pushing and pulling her,
    we will make her breathe a little
    if we can, my sweet sister.   24,252
MAGDALENE O holy and worthy creature
    and the most blessed of all women,
    now we lose your son Jesus,
    my gentle master, my sweet friend,   24,256
    without whom we have absolutely nothing
    and live under the shadow of Death;
    if by unfortunate chance we must
    lose you with him,   24,260
    may Death pierce my heart heavy
    with the pain tormenting it.
GRIFFON Walk, villain!
CLAQUEDENT I think he sleeps.
    How he staggers!   24,264
ORILLART While going forth, he saw
    his cronies weeping so hard
    and became so discouraged
    that I think he'll stay behind.   24,268
PILATE Why don't you chase them away?
    They seem like mad women.
BRAYART Go away, damned old women
    or you'll receive hard blows   24,272
    so well placed on your backs
    that we won't have to do it again.
SAINT JOHN We can no longer accompany him,
    my ladies, you see the situation.   24,276
MAGDALENE Alas, John, we will not leave
    Mary, your honorable aunt,

who follows him in such anguish
that no heart ever endured more misery.   24,280
MARY JACOBI If it pleases God, we will lead her
as long as she would like to walk.
BROYEFORT We do nothing but plod on.
I can't stop worrying.   24,284
We should have hanged four
since the time we left.
PILATE Are you stuck to this spot?
Soldiers, move on a little.   24,288
GRIFFON He can bear no more as you see.
Must we keep repeating it?
CLAQUEDENT He has completely halted here
and will die crossing the fields.   24,292
CENTURION Procurator, you're wasting your time
chasing him so. Alas, you see he's so tired
that we can no longer inflict pain
nor any other tribulation without his suffering death.   24,296
Look at the load he's carrying.
There is no creature so strong
and with such fierce courage
who would not have had enough with half   24,300
the load he's carrying.
Even though he is so enfeebled
that he only awaits death to take him,
order that we wait a bit   24,304
to provide him relief.
PILATE You speak wisely Centurion.
If he's carrying a load and a heavy weight,
I'm not the one responsible;   24,308
the Jews are, who hold him in disgrace.
What do you think we should do?
We will consider what you say.
CENTURION I'll tell you what we will do   24,312
to avoid greater harm.
Here is a village peasant
coming here to the city;
we must   24,316
load him with this cross.
I think that if he carries it,
Christ will go, seeing that it is not
much further to mount Calvary.   24,320
This will be a great comfort to him.
PILATE He's a big and strong enough fellow

to support such a burden.
Go, Griffon, go summon him   24,324
and tell him to come and do
a little job.
GRIFFON Gladly.
I'll tell him everything to the letter.   24,328

[*He goes toward Simon.*]

Come here, come, good sir;
you must follow our path.
Hey, hey, good fellow, can't you hear?
Come talk to our lords.   24,332
SIMON OF CYRENE I have enough to listen to elsewhere. °
I must tend to my business.
ORILLART Must this villain grumble?
Come on scoundrel! You will come!   24,336
SIMON OF CYRENE Ah, my lords, you'll have to wait
until I finish my business.
GRIFFON We will certainly not wait.
You'll come very quickly.   24,340
SIMON OF CYRENE Alas, what do you ask of me,
you who force me by such means?
ORILLART Your shoulders will know it well
before you return, don't worry.   24,344
GRIFFON Sir, I entrust and give
this good fellow into your hands.
CENTURION Come here and speak to me, villain.
You go idling through the fields   24,348
like a wicked adventurer.
You must be put to work.
SIMON OF CYRENE Alas, my lords, what will I do?
You have so frightened me   24,352
that I have neither heart nor will
nor limb that can lift a thing;
and if you wish to harm me,
I appeal for my safety.   24,356
CENTURION No, good man, you risk nothing.

24,333–96 Simon of Cyrene is mentioned in Matthew 27:31–32, Mark 15:20–21, and
Luke 23:26. The latter two passages specify that Simon was coming in from the
country. In Marcadé, Christ asks to be relieved of the cross. In Gréban, he shows
no such weakness; the Centurion proposes that Simon relieve him. In Marcadé,
Simon the Leper carries the cross (lines 15,917–71).

But to support this Jesus,
who can no longer carry his cross
and stays here without assistance, 24,360
you must, to help him,
carry this cross yourself.
SIMON OF CYRENE Ah my lords, forgive me,
I will never do it for anything, 24,364
for I'll be so reproached
that in all my days I'll never have honor.
You know the great dishonor
it is to carry a cross today. 24,368
I would certainly rather
die than perform such a task.
GRIFFON You slothful, lazy old rogue,
full of rebellion. 24,372
You'll do it whether you want to or not!
Quickly, take up the burden!
SIMON OF CYRENE I protest!
ORILLART Do it, villain! 24,376
Are you backing off?
SIMON OF CYRENE If you wrong me and I am not guilty,
I protest!
BROYART Do it, villain! 24,380
You'll get so many strong blows,
that we'll break your jaw.
SIMON OF CYRENE I protest!
CLAQUEDENT Do it, villain! 24,384
Are you backing off?
BROYEFORT You seek to escape in vain.
You must submit.

[*They relieve Jesus of the cross.*]

SIMON OF CYRENE Let's go then, since it is so.
I'll do your will,
but in truth, the shame that you cause me
is very painful. 24,388
Jesus, the most holy and the best
of all the prophets,
you come to a pitiful end,
given your virtuous life. 24,392
For your death I must carry
your hard and shameful cross;
if this is wrong, I impute
those who judged you. 24,396

[They put Jesus' cross on his shoulders.]

GRIFFON My lords, he is loaded well.
    Let's get quickly on the road.
SALMANASAR I have a great desire to see him
    affixed to this high tabernacle   24,400
    to know if there will be a miracle
    that can bring him down.
CENTURION Soldiers, hasten along this Jesus
    and the two thieves at his sides.   24,404
    If they resist, then beat them
    so well that there is nothing to reproach.
CLAQUEDENT There is no difficulty in that, sir.
    We're doing all we can.   24,408
GOD THE FATHER Pity must move all hearts
    to piteously lament
    the martyrdom and great torment
    that Jesus, my dear son, endures.   24,412
    He feels such immense anguish,
    that, since the world has existed,
    no one has ever endured greater,
    which cannot last longer   24,416
    without his suffering a shameful death.
    And his holy body will only last
    until he has suffered through it,
    it seems, for he goes on enduring   24,420
    and suffering torment
    without any comfort to relieve him.
    Thus it is fitting that Death shorten it
    and prepare to execute him   24,424
    to satisfy the request
    of the proud lady Justice
    who, despite prayers and pleas,
    does not wish to give up any of her rights.   24,428
    Michael, go therefore and comfort
    during his bitter Passion,
    my son, who is full of charity,
    my child, my most beloved offspring,   24,432
    who will extend his soft flesh
    across the powerful tree of the cross.
MICHAEL Father of heaven and king of kings,
    humbly, in a modest manner,   24,436
    your good and just will
    shall be realized and accomplished.

SATAN   King of hell, who wear the crown
of the horrible, infernal abyss,   24,440
our affair is going so badly
that our whole chasm is destroyed.
LUCIFER   By what means?
SATAN   I accomplished nothing.
This Jesus is given over to death   24,444
and could not be freed
by any means I tried.
And yet, I tried with great effort
to tempt Pilate's wife,   24,448
but the disloyal babble
of the Jews never ceased,
and they pressed upon Pilate so much
that he sentenced him to death.   24,452
LUCIFER   Ah cursed Satan, go hang yourself
on a gibbet of burning fire,
since you did not better preserve
the rights and laws of the house!   24,456
Go, dragon, go, cruel serpent,
and keep a lookout again
in case by an unfortunate chance
the rest could escape.   24,460
SATAN   It's done. Don't think about it anymore.
There is no one who could have delayed it.
We only need to guard well
our entrances and our doors with force,   24,464
so that, at least if he forces himself in,
we can resist him.
LUCIFER   Cerberus.
CERBERUS   I hear ya, *magister*.
LUCIFER   And you, my devils, are you sleeping?   24,468
Bar our entrances with great bolts. °
Keep our portals firmly shut
and stay in front of them
in great armies to protect them,   24,472
for you will soon see
our enemy make his assault.
CERBERUS   Have no fear. If he enters,
May my muzzle be burned.   24,476
FERGALUS   All is well-barred;

24,469 This command is found in *The Gospel of Nicodemus*.

how then would he enter?

ASTAROTH He'll have to be more clever
    than all of us devils together.   24,480
    Now, by my hook, I think
    he'll stay here, if he comes.

SATAN Master, we don't know if he's coming;
    You take care of things here   24,484
    and, to see how things turn out,
    I'll go on an expedition.

LUCIFER So that your path may be shortened,
    may the devil guide you.   24,488

MICHAEL *Here he returns to the cross.*
    Son of God, upon whom all the angels
    take joy in gazing,
    and whose perfect nobility
    no mouth could describe,   24,492
    who to redeem humankind
    have offered your precious body
    and suffered so many horrible torments
    that only God knows the number,   24,496
    and all this to take man from the shadow
    of death and bring him to rest,
    and who with this intention still,
    wish for death in order to receive humankind,   24,500
    achieve and realize your duty
    and make your will manifestly
    obedient to God, your father,
    who will make an offering of this   24,504
    holy sacrifice to lady Justice,
    one more acceptable than any other,
    greatly revered and pleasing
    in its sweet perfume.   24,508
    Once the cross was held in great dishonor
    and in great scorn
    and was cursed by everyone.
    Now its name shall be revered,   24,512
    exalted, and celebrated
    through this most glorious distinction.
    Once it was said to be ignominious
    and all the people whose bodies   24,516
    were hanged on it were damned.
    Now it will be stained with your blood
    through which death will be conquered
    and hell overthrown.   24,520

Here Michael along with some other angels stays with Jesus Christ.

RUBION Now we have walked so fast
    that we have climbed with great torment
    the mountain of Calvary
    with a large company.   24,524

PILATE Come on, soldiers, perverse troop,
    must you celebrate now?
    You should have prepared for your task
    when you stopped here.   24,528
    Where are the three crosses?

GRIFFON Here they are.
    We'll bring each to you right away.
    These are for the two thieves   24,532
    and this one is for the hypocrite.

CAIAPHAS Without waiting any further, °
    the reason why we hang
    Jesus in this manner
    must be written on it.   24,536

PILATE Your request is easy enough.
    Here is a plaque all ready,
    on which I'll write it, if you wish,
    and then we'll attach it   24,540
    to the cross.

ANNAS We beg you to
    consent to do it.

JEROBOAM Procurator, I want to point out to you
    that, if we are wise, it will be good   24,544
    to write it in various languages,
    so that at least, foreign
    passers-by do not pass without
    understanding what it means.   24,548

PILATE Do not doubt but that it will be written
    with very great ingenuity.

GRIFFON My lords, all is ready,
    the crosses along with the ropes and nails. 24,552
    Therefore decide among yourselves
    which one you want us to start with.

CAIAPHAS According to my thinking, it seems
    that the quicker the better   24,556
    in killing this babbler

24,533–50 *Passion d'Arras* (lines 16,187–272).

because the sooner we have him die,
the sooner we rejoice.
He has waited too long already.   24,560
GRIFFON Do you want him hanged
all dressed or in his undergarment?
ANNAS Neither. That's not the plan
to which we agreed.   24,564
We want him to be stripped
as naked as an earthworm
and at no prayer or request
are you to leave him, above or below,   24,568
a large, medium, or small piece of cloth
with which he could cover a single spot.
ORILLART You want him to be the same as when
he came from his mother's womb?   24,572
JEROBOAM Exactly.
GRIFFON It is a great affront;
nevertheless, whether honorable or blameworthy,
you will have it.
BRAYART He's so dishonorable
that we cannot mistreat him enough.   24,576
CLAQUEDENT Let's hurry without saying another word.
Here, villain, come to the feast.
Neither your ass nor your head
will stay covered.   24,580
This garment here is poorly opened.
I've never seen any of its kind.
BROYEFORT Why?
CLAQUEDENT It is all of one piece,
woven from top to bottom.   24,584
BROYEFORT Don't worry. No, take it off him.
It'll be for our spoils.
Extend your arms, vile dog.
Let yourself be undressed a bit.   24,588

Here they strip him naked

OUR LADY Alas, who will be able to advise me
and rouse me from my heavy sorrow
in which my poor heart drowns
and is on the verge of perishing,   24,592
if Death should come to kill it?
I seek Death, and it denies me.
Ah, my son, when I held you,
I took all my joy from you   24,596

~ 127 ~

and all good, in order to be one with you.
Now I lose you in a piteous way,
now I must see your death.
Son, I cannot forget you.   24,600
My sisters, I would like to beseech you
in the name of God the triumphant,
that we approach my child
and pass through this crowd.   24,604
MARY JACOBI We will not leave you, my kind sister,
whatever the torment or distress,
but wherever you walk,
we will follow you with good heart.   24,608
MARY SALOME Look there, my gentle sister,
at the greatest pity that ever was.
They have already prepared the wood
where he must be led to death.   24,612
They have stripped him so completely naked
that there is not the least thing on his body.
OUR LADY O false, incorrigible people,
O immense betrayal,   24,616
which leads you at its will,
you have offended honor too much,
and it is indeed separated from you.
The madness of envy sweeps you away.   24,620
Harsh people of cruel rule,
take pity on human nature.
If you had considered honor,
you would not have been so villainous   24,624
as to strip him so completely.
You have dishonored him too much.

Our Lady puts a cloth in front of Jesus while saying these lines.

Alas, my noble child,
my dear and indispensable treasure,   24,628
of the gentlest and kindest character
that was ever born under the heavens,
spontaneous motherly love
compels me to come cover you,   24,632
and if I could have done more for you,
God knows it would have been done with a good heart.
But no, they want to destroy you,
and wrong your mother so greatly   24,636
as to kill and give her dear son over
to death in front of her eyes.

What sorrow, what a piteous exemplar!
My son, let it not displease you   24,640
if, at parting, as my whole reward,
I kiss you, since I cannot do better.
CENTURION Griffon, you really are a stupid old swine
because you don't make these women go away.   24,644
GRIFFON Hop over the barrier,
quarrelsome women; you must do this
or you will get it on your snout.
May all the devils take part.   24,648
ORILLART Now, lords, stand aside
to see how we work
and if we crucify him
as you wish it.   24,652
MARDOCEE It's good that you stretch him out
on the ground and fully attach him
before placing him upright.
You'll find it easier.   24,656
CAIAPHAS The idea is not bad;
then they can work better.
BRAYART You don't have to think about it anymore.
We'll do it that way.   24,660
Come on villain, lie here.
Your filthy carcass must
be immediately worked upon
to your bloody affliction.   24,664

[They lay Jesus flat on the cross.]

GRIFFON First I'll attach his arms
so that the business speeds up.
Rogue, extend this paw.
I'm going to tie you so tight   24,668
that you won't be able to untie yourself.
Broyefort, what use are you there?
What did you do with the nails?
BROYEFORT There they are,
right next to you. Can't you see anything?   24,672
GRIFFON But must they be thrown
in my face? What a gentleman!
Now give me that hammer
and then you'll see my muscle.   24,676
ORILLART Strike it right into him.
GRIFFON I will,
if you'd just let me do it.

Here is the roughest nail   24,680
that I've ever encountered.
CLAQUEDENT You had them forged without points,
so they enter a little more awkwardly.
GRIFFON It holds so well and tightly   24,684
that nobody could remove it.
BROYEFORT I wanted to amuse myself by
nailing his other hand to this side,
but there's a distance of three fingers
from the palm to the hole;   24,688
as a result, I can't attach him
unless somebody shows me how.
GRIFFON You're nothing but a clumsy oaf. °
Let me do it by myself.   24,692
I'll make it reach
or no vein will remain whole.
BRAYART Now show us the method
to see if we agree with it.   24,696
GRIFFON Take these two big cords
which I tied around his fist
and you four, pull as much as you can,
even if the sinews break,   24,700
until you make the hand reach
the hole made for it.
CLAQUEDENT The idea is very good,
blessed be he who gives it.   24,704
GRIFFON Now pull hard, hard, scoundrels! °
The hand's getting there, or almost.
BROYEFORT I must not fail.
Now pull hard!   24,708
BRAYART Hard, scoundrels!
I'm afraid his heart might fail him
because of the pulling.
CLAQUEDENT What do we care?
Now pull hard!
GRIFFON Hard scoundrels!
The hand's getting there, or almost.   24,712
ORILLART Is it still coming?
GRIFFON It's just about there.

24,691 *hours de Sçavoye.* Literally, "a bear from Savoie."
24,705–32 *Passion d'Arras* (lines 16,106–50). In Marcadé, Jews, not Romans,
perform these actions.

Now hammer the nail in.
A bent crossbow never
stretched better than this. 24,716
BANNANIAS The rogue says nothing nor makes a sound,
no matter what you do.
GRIFFON Look, the two are very well attached;
let's quickly move to the feet. 24,720
ELYACHIM We must cross them one over the other
to do the job more quickly.
GRIFFON First here's a problem,
We're failing completely. 24,724
ELYACHIM How?
GRIFFON The feet are so far away
that they can't be pulled
to the hole.
NAASON They must be pulled
in the same way, neither more nor less, 24,728
as you did with his hands.
By this method you'll make them reach;
don't you understand?
GRIFFON You'll see it done
as soon as I've knotted my cord. 24,732
MAGDALENE O pity, O mercy,
O sweet Jesus to whom every sinner
is reconciled through the remission of sins,
sweet fountain of harmony, 24,736
when I remember your noble deeds,
I see they're making an unjust exaction.
MARY JACOBI False and perverse nation
full of obstinacy, 24,740
how did you dare think
of sending to execution
the one who, for your salvation,
has always toiled without cease. 24,744
MARY SALOME In the end you will be punished for it,
false and cursed progeny,
and this has already been indicated to you.
Race united in all evildoing 24,748
and devoid of all honor,
you have taken away all our good.
SAINT JOHN O fountain of charity,
light without darkness, 24,752
you leave our company
in such great confusion

that, in truth, all joy
has departed from our hearts. 24,756
GRIFFON Our work has been done very well.
May Jupiter be praised!
I believe he is so well nailed
that he will never leave alive. 24,760
ORILLART Never did the string of a bow stretch
better than his sinews, both weak and strong.
One could count one by one
the bones there in his body. 24,764
BRAYART I'm looking up and down to see
if the nails are holding well.
GRIFFON Now then, go try his teeth.
See how you can get them. 24,768
PILATE Come on, come on, leave off this foolishness.
Since the writing is attached,
make sure that the tree is fixed
and everywhere secure. 24,772
No more clowning around.
Prepare the crosses and the crucifix,
so that these Jews who have tormented him so much
are satisfied. 24,776
BROYEFORT He will soon be lifted upright
into the air, quite ashamed and confounded.
PILATE Take lances, swords,
guisarmes, pick-axes, standards, 24,780
ladders, tents, and javelins.
Each soldier should lend a hand
and support his side
with great and effective strength. 24,784
Heave!
GRIFFON Heave!
CLAQUEDENT Pull the wood.
ORILLART Pull!
Give support there.
BRAYART Support it.
The whole thing is falling on us.
Heave! 24,788
BROYEFORT Heave!
GRIFFON Pull the wood!
CLAQUEDENT Pull!
I've never had such a heavy load!
I'll break a bone if you don't pick it up.
Heave!

ORILLART Heave!

BRAYART Pull the wood!

BROYEFORT Pull!
    Support it!   24,792

GRIFFON Give support there!

CENTURION Ah, comrades, you suffer
    and take great pains,
    but you'll receive good payment
    as soon as you return.   24,796

CLAQUEDENT We are so well equipped
    and have done so much that there he is.

ORILLART Come what may, he is up.
    We can definitely leave.   24,800

BRAYART The devil can take him
    for all the trouble he gave us!

BROYEFORT I don't care
    if he doesn't take him or if he does carry him off.   24,804
    Let's see if the cross is straight
    and then prop it up from the bottom.

GRIFFON And you there, Jesus? Are you enjoying yourself?
    You're honored now! Are you comfortable?   24,808
    If you please, preach to us here about
    your good works in the old days.

ANNAS Procurator, we do not quite understand °
    the reason for this placque,   24,812
    and if I am not mistaken
    it should not be as it is.
    You put the inscription
    in three languages as I see,   24,816
    "Jesus of Nazareth, the king
    of the Jews." You have written it thus.
    However, it does not read correctly
    and is to our great detriment.   24,820

CAIAPHAS Great error exists in the writing,
    and it should not say
    that he is king, but that he calls himself so
    against the law and in great error,   24,824
    for which he incurred
    the punishment of death, as is evident.

JACOB He speaks truly; our honor is lost by it.
    Procurator, it is not good as it stands.   24,828

24,811–32 The fullest account of Pilate's sign is found in John 19:19–22.

PILATE My lords, *quod scripsi scripsi* °
and whoever wants to grumble may do so,
for what I have written here
is done, and the writing will stay.   24,832
JORAM Be sure then that it will cause
the confusion of all,
for all men who read it
will think less well of us.   24,836
PILATE I can do no more. Let it satisfy you that
I complied with you too much.
It still weighs heavily on me
that I was burdened with this.   24,840
GRIFFON Since Jesus is dispensed with,
tell us what to do next.
CENTURION Crucify these two thieves
in the position that they should be placed,   24,844
one to the right, the other to the left;
I think that is their plan.
ISACAR You're right, Centurion.
We want them put there.   24,848
GRIFFON They will soon be well placed,
since they have been given into my hands;
They will soon be disposed of
and hanged on two beautiful gibbets.   24,852
Come here, evil thieves,
cursed by God and Nature.
Here is your sepulchre,
you will never be able to escape it.   24,856
DYMAS If we must fade away in death
and be subjected to the cross,
we must not complain nor moan,
for we have well deserved it.   24,860
GESTAS We have ended up too badly
to be used for any good.
ORILLART It's from having served a bad master °
that one receives such harsh payment.   24,864
BRAYART Whoever must hang, cannot drown °
if the gibbet doesn't go swimming.

24,829 *Quod scripsi scripsi.* John 19:22, "What I have written, I have written."
24,863–64 *C'est ung mauvais maistre servy / dont on reçoit si dur loyer.* A proverb
(Jodogne, 448).
24,865 *Qui doit pendre, il ne puet noier.* A proverb (Hassell 178).

That's a miserable saying;
everyone must know it.   24,868
GRIFFON You keep chattering away
and without helping me even a little.
CLAQUEDENT We come rushing.
Come, comrades, let each one get to work.   24,872
Let's hang these two thieves in a row
in the way that pleases our lords.
BROYEFORT Also Jesus is all alone.
He's only waiting for company.   24,876
GRIFFON He'll soon be well furnished with it,
and with people of high quality.
Here's a lout as false
as you'll find from here to Pamplona.   24,880
ORILLART He's not worth a prune;
he's from the same kettle of fish.
GRIFFON Help me get them ready,
and then we'll place them above.   24,884

Here they tie them to the crosses and meanwhile Satan speaks.
When they are tied, the soldiers raise them up without speaking

SATAN All my understanding dissolves
and is devoured by furious rage
because I hatched a plot
that exceeds all my skill,   24,888
and I could not rectify it
when I thought to delay him.
Once through a clever trick
I caused the world to fall in ruin   24,892
and be banished from divine glory
through woman and deception,
and now I thought I could prevent
its redemption through a woman.   24,896
But it's not worth talking about.
I have completely failed,
for the Jews' hearts are formed of
such cruel and strong envy   24,900
that Jesus must suffer death.
There he is, already crucified;
the devil guided me well,
and I wasted my time in   24,904
cooking up such a bad stew
that will cause us a great loss.
What will the savage troop of the damned

~ 135 ~

say when they learn of this? 24,908
What laments, what hideous cries there will be,
if through great strength
he despoils the hideous prison
of its ancient inhabitants. 24,912
It would be better to be delivered to the dogs
than to find myself in such a mob.
I will still stay here
and will not leave quite so soon 24,916
but will remain here
near this cursed cross
to see the end and the behavior
that this Jesus will exhibit. 24,920
When his soul departs,
if I can get my paw on it,
it will come with me,
tired and dispirited, to the dark place. 24,924
PILATE Are those two unfortunates hanged?
Companions, are they disposed of?
CENTURION Answer, presumptuous fools,
are those two unfortunates hanged? 24,928
GRIFFON Since I tied that scoundrel,
you'll no longer be inconvenienced.
JEROBOAM Are those two unfortunates hanged?
Companions, are they disposed of? 24,932
ORILLART I think they're affixed
and hang so well at their ease,
that if they should ever descend
they'll really know some tricks. 24,936
EMILIUS Jesus, you babbled in vain,
for you're in a pretty situation.
Look at the noble entourage
by which you are accompanied. 24,940
CELSIDON You're hardly overworked.
Preach a few words if you must.
You'll be heard from afar,
for you're lodged high enough. 24,944
RABANUS Now descend from there if you can °
and jump right here in the middle;
In the past you made yourself the son of God;

24,945–48 Matthew 27:40; Mark 15:30; *Passion d'Arras* (lines 16,537–40). In both
Marcadé and Gréban, Jews mock Christ on the cross.

come down in that faith.   24,948

NENBROTH He doesn't hear that speech.
    He has other things to think about.
    May God protect this king of drivelers,
    the seducer of Galilee,   24,952
    who with all his might has abolished
    and destroyed our law!

SALMANASAR He need not be reminded of that anymore,
    since he's doing his penance.   24,956

PHARES He is a prophet of ignorance.
    If he had known future things,
    he would have avoided from early on
    the pains that press so hard on him.   24,960
    But no. It's right that he should cry
    and regret his former pleasures.

JESUS *primum verbum*
    Pater mi, dimitte illis, °
    nam nesciunt quid faciunt.   24,964
    Father, who elected your servants,
    in whose hands are all things,
    you see by what kind of people I am taken;
    they pitilessly destroy me;   24,968
    forgive them if they have done wrong,
    for they know not what they do.

DYMAS O worthy citizens
    of the noble land, Judea,   24,972
    you see the lamentable ways
    of death which has already come to seek us.
    I have truly deserved it, I know.
    My sin constrains and wrings me.   24,976
    Pray to God that from among his noble graces
    he will grant us the gift of mercy.

GESTAS O terrible, furious Death,
    your arrow will soon strike me,   24,980
    and it is not worth being alive.
    Not a soul will come to my rescue.
    God, have you given me such a destiny
    as the one that will soon come upon me?   24,984
    Cursed be the day that ever

24,963–64 Luke 23:34, "Father, forgive them, for they know not what they do."
Meditations on the Life of Christ (336) divides Christ's utterances on the cross into
seven "words."

my father engendered me!

NACHOR It is appropriate to greet
    our Christ who is so wise.   24,988
    Look at him in the face,
    my lords, your most pitiable king,
    the bloody presumptuous fool
    who has done us so much harm.   24,992

NATHAN Does he now hold his assembly of barons
    and his grand court between those two?
    Look at him in the face,
    my lords, your most pitiable king.   24,996

JACOB He is a noble dignitary
    to make a truly majestic king.
    I don't know of what heritage he is,
    unless he's king of the unfortunates.   25,000

ISACAR These are titles of high nobility.
    But as a king, who prides himself on them,
    does he now hold his assembly of barons
    and his grand court between those two?   25,004

JEROBOAM Fie on the evil, dangerous fool
    who wanted to tell the people
    of his ability to destroy the temple
    and rebuild it in three days.   25,008

MARDOCEE You wished to trust too much
    your false art; I am a witness to this,
    for now that you need help,
    the devil, whom you served,   25,012
    lets you undergo death,
    so that there is no magic art
    nor evil that you can use
    in order to escape.   25,016

NAASON Thus the enemy knows how to trick
    those who use such deceit.
    Now where is your Beelzebub, °
    by whose power you expelled   25,020
    the other enemies of the body?
    In what place is he hiding?

ELYACHIM He awaits him at the bottom of hell
    to burn in the eternal fire.   25,024
    Consider, Jesus, if your evil

25,019–21 This charge is found in the Gospel of Nicodemus and in the *Passion d'Arras* (lines 15,564–65).

or your malice that was so ready
now abounds in your head.
Did you think you would always reign?   25,028
Did you think you would always wage
war against the synagogue?
Did you think you would be so formidable
that we could not injure you?   25,032
BANNANIAS Go, go preach and babble
against our laws and our decrees!
Go reveal our secrets
to please the common people!   25,036
See if they have come here
to free you from our hands!
We stay sound and you remain
for death, for your destruction.   25,040
JOATHAN Is this the noble champion,
the powerful Emmanuel
who was to reign in Israel?
Is this the noble treasure   25,044
whose coming to the world
the prophets confidently announced?
May God and Nature confound him!
He is not worthy of such a name   25,048
nor of such honor.
ANNAS I believe not
and truly think he becomes more moderate
and considers his misdeeds,
through which he deceived the people.   25,052
ROILLART Is this the crafty worker,
the artist of wonderful tools,
who in three days was to build
a high and massive temple?   25,056
DENTART He's too badly positioned there
to achieve it soon.
GADIFFER Tell me, crazy madman, are you the one °
who spread the boast   25,060
of destroying the work
of Solomon's noble temple?
I think you'll do it
soon, provided we let you.   25,064
MALCUIDANT If he wants to make a new one

25,059–64 Matthew 27:40; Mark 15:29–30; and *Passion d'Arras* (lines 16,535–36).

in three days as he boasted,
he's well equipped to do it.
Jesus, make a new temple   25,068
right away; for in place of a hammer, °
you have big nails with long points
with which your filthy hands are fastened;
and in place of wood to work with,   25,072
you can use the gibbet
which stretches out your sinews and veins.
DRAGON Where are your vain tricks,
Jesus, and your enchantments?   25,076
GUEULU You who are feeling such severe pain,
where are your vain tricks?
BRAYART Your works were not sound;
we see this in the end,   25,080
and if you uphold them, you lie,
because, for them, you suffer such pains.
ESTONNÉ Where are your vain tricks
Jesus, and your enchantments?   25,084
We see that the artifices
with which you pretended to perform miracles
on the dead and the possessed
did not have a good foundation,   25,088
but were falsely done
by enormous and hideous devils.
It is evident, because, even in your own case,
you cannot find the means   25,092
to free and save yourself,
but let yourself die in shame.
MALABRUN In the end you are worthless,
Jesus, you and your stinking group.   25,096
MAUCOURANT Prophet, do you hear what I tell you?
In the end, you are worthless.
JEROBOAM Your talk means nothing to him;
he's drunk too much villainy.   25,100
EMILIUS In the end, you are worthless
Jesus, you, and your stinking group.
If your stinking mouth denies it
and wants to contest it,   25,104
descend from there and come down below;
then we'll consider your strength certain.

25,069–70 The same sarcastic comment is found in the *Passion Isabeau* (l. 3,250).

CELSIDON He doesn't have the time.

RABANUS It's not the right moment;
    he must be thinking of other things. 25,108

GRIFFON If you can do anything, get to it.

NENBROTH He doesn't have the time.

ORILLART It's not the right moment.
    If he knows a way, I assure you
    he'll get out of it sooner or later. 25,112

SALMANASAR He doesn't have the time.

CLAQUEDENT It's not the right moment;
    he must be thinking of other things.

GESTAS Jesus, don't you have any concern for
    the obvious peril you're in? 25,116
    Have you become so stupid?
    Don't you see death awaiting you?
    Everyone strives to kill you.
    It's no wonder it doesn't move you, 25,120
    for a wise man, who understands his fate,
    escapes death when he can.

DYMAS O evil and unfortunate man,
    in whom all good has perished, 25,124
    doesn't Jesus carry enough of a burden
    without your insulting him further?
    With such badly chosen words
    you censure him too much, 25,128
    and you don't change your situation at all,
    you who are on the verge of damnation.

GESTAS Come on scoundrel, are you so desirous °
    of dying here before everyone? 25,132
    Don't you see our great suffering,
    if we aren't saved by him?
    If you are Christ
    descended for the sake of human nature, 25,136
    why don't you save yourself and us,
    who are here dying such a villainous death?

DYMAS Wretched man of low morality,
    you do great wrong in insulting him. 25,140
    If we die for our offense,
    we have deserved such recompense.

25,131–58 Matthew 27:44 and Mark 15:32. Luke 23:39–43 tells of a good thief and a bad one. Their names and a fuller account are found in *The Gospel of Nicodemus*; see also *Passion d'Arras* (lines 16,577–625).

But he, who is without sin,
holy and just in his innocence, 25,144
dies wrongly, without having done any foolishness,
and whoever offends him further does great wrong.
We have deserved death,
and he never did wrong. 25,148
There is only evil in our lives,
and he always did only good.
O sweet Jesus, whom I love and worship,
in whom I have perfect trust, 25,152
if you go to your kingdom,
remember my plight.

JESUS *secundum verbum* I tell you with certainty
that, because of the desire I see in you, 25,156
you will be placed with me
this day in paradise.

DYMAS My savior, my sovereign king,
in this desirable anticipation, 25,160
I receive death patiently.
May God grant that it be blessed!

OUR LADY Deeply constrained sadness, °
how can I withstand you? 25,164
Where will I go?
What will I do?
What will I say?
I feel so much anguish 25,168
that my heart is breaking.
I do not know
if the trial
that I am undergoing 25,172
has just begun
or if it is ending.
If Death which disperses
and separates everything 25,176
takes me for its portion,
my sorrow and my languishing life
will depart.
If life keeps me, 25,180
let Death not consider
passing judgment.
I begin late

25,163–356 A complaint by the Virgin at the foot of the cross (Sinclair, 260).

my immeasurable suffering. 25,184
O cruelty made more cruel,
Death marked by a painful bite,
how much delayed is your sojourn with
the sad and weeping woman 25,188
who looks to nothing but her end.
You are really indeed terrible
and full of such cruelty
when you see me ready 25,192
and separated from all good,
why do you not strike me with your dart?
False Death of terrible vigilance,
it is your contemptible condition 25,196
to be always lazy and slothful
with those whose lives are long to them,
those who, weeping, call you without cease.
Your eye looks at those 25,200
whom the world watches over the most,
and who seek defense against you,
and in their heart's depth, you pierce them
so severely that they fall dying. 25,204
Do the same to me: you see me laboring
in fierce suffering that rushes upon me,
and you do not want to get rid of
these pitiful remains. 25,208
My son, my son, I want to admonish you.
My sweet child, my blessed reward,
is it good to forget one's mother
in such a manner? 25,212
Look at me, son, I pray you,
acknowledge your dearest mother
who because of you has such a sorrowful expression
in piteous lamentation. 25,216
Jesus, my son, my gracious child,
my son, Jesus, my precious treasure,
is this how the separation between us is to be?
O separation 25,220
shared in great torment and sorrow,
O affliction and painful sorrow of the accused,
the mother is separated from the son by death,
what harsh torment! 25,224
Son, consider this terrible death
or if you must die because of envy,
at least let us die together!

I want it so.   25,228
Son, grant me the desire of my will;
living without you will be only sorrow to me,
in dying with you I will never lament nor sorrow.
This is my gain.   25,232
I don't care about a shameful death,
it is enough for me; I want no death but this.
I beseech you my dear child,
grant me this request.   25,236
One body, one blood, and one life
demand to be ravished by one death.
We are thus. You do not deny it.
I know it well.   25,240
We are one body, for yours is from mine.
I hold your pure blood engendered by me.
Now if it flows until there is nothing,
O what distress!   25,244
Thus I lose my treasure, my wealth,
if death overtakes you and leaves me.
Ah, cruel Death, turn your cruelty to me,
make everything the same   25,248
without separating what is so united;
or leave everything; he is punished enough;
or take my son and seize me with him,
I'll be happy.   25,252
Death, spiteful with cruel spite,
Death, sorrowing with mournful sorrow,
bold Death, outrageous boldness,
do you want to disjoin   25,256
the couple that love meant to join together,
separating one and piercing the other with your dart?
Unite both, either pierce or release both.
Son, it will not do so.   25,260
Let Death do the worst it can,
hang your body as high as it would like,
but it can never separate me from you,
however hard it tries.   25,264
If your body hangs on that high cross,
there hangs my soul, which out of pity takes me there,
and there is not a wound on you so painful
that I do not feel it.   25,268
Son, your pain is fresh in my heart.
I grieve for the pain that overwhelms and kills you,
but I fear much more lest death carry you off

before me.   25,272
O cruel Death, I am defiant of you.
I defy you; I do not acknowledge your power.
Make me undergo the hardest trial
that you can arrange.   25,276
Leave my son; you will do a great act of charity.
Make me die; you will be very sweet to me.
You will reduce the greatest sorrow
that ever existed.   25,280
Blessed son, courteous son,
gracious son, most moral son,
the best formed body among the living,
O pure beauty,   25,284
choice of humans, flower of all nature,
rich coloring, perfect image,
pitiful look, sweetest countenance,
sacred face,   25,288
glowing face nobly shaped,
are you disfigured there,
with dim eyes crimsoned in blood?
Harsh dealings!   25,292
Son, are you such? I no longer recognize you.
Son, is it you who are placing yourself in this situation,
giving yourself to the cross, submitting to death
without deserving it?   25,296
Bold Death, do you want to take away my son,
undermine my fort, demolish my treasure?
This is life. Do you dare attack it?
Deaf Death,   25,300
quick to harm, bold in doing evil.
Alas, my son, I must say it,
this evil, this sorrow, this great sickness
comes to you because of me,   25,304
because of me you feel pain,
because of me you suffer, because of me death befalls you.
Pain, suffering, all this happens to you
through the weakness   25,308
of having taken your humanity in me.
For if it were removed and if your divinity,
holding the second position in the Trinity,
were liberated,   25,312
it would remain for you only to reign and live,
feel joy and pursue perfect glory.
Humanity delivers you to the death

to which you come.   25,316
Therefore, my son, this is all that you have from me:
suffering, weakness, pain which you take
and fatal death to which you come.
And from you I have   25,320
joy, health, honor, and all good things
from which I receive sustenance and live.
Therefore, my son, if I have part in your unique good,
suffer me to take part in your pains,   25,324
for the greatest ones are the most important to me.
Let us die as one; otherwise if I fail,
you will do me wrong.   25,328
O my child, consider my situation;
give me my share without deliberating.
I have a part in you if you manage it well,
much more fecund   25,332
than other mothers, more precious and pure,
for they have only one part in the children
they bring into the world; the father has the second.
You are all mine;   25,336
no mortal man can claim anything.
If you have a father, he is celestial.
Therefore, my son, in God's name, take care
not to abandon recklessly   25,340
in your agony
my right, my share, my blood, and my nature.
If this happens, then I protest
the cruel separation.   25,344
Perverse Jews, in whom a branch of death resides,
traitorous dogs, I protest against you.
Do you gain in value today by betraying such a person?
All of you answer.   25,348
Alas, my son, I turn to you,
see my sorrow, my grievous suffering,
and with your eyes so precious and sweet
look at the woman   25,352
who conceived you, pure virgin and maiden,
who nourished you with her tender breast,
and tell me of my mortal pain
that more remains.   25,356
JESUS *tertium verbum*

Mulier, ecce filius tuus. °
Woman, take heart and have patience,
cease this sorrow. If I am pierced by death,
accept this son whom I give you,   25,360
your nephew who will care well for
you after my painful death.
Take her, John, I appoint her your mother. °
Watch over her well and do not leave her.   25,364
SAINT JOHN   Alas, when I consider my position,
my master and my most sweet lord,
you do me a very great honor
to commend your mother   25,368
to me and to command me
to regard her as mistress and mother.
Please God that it never happen,
no matter how great the danger, that I abandon   25,372
my mother and dear mistress.
I will gladly accompany her
and regard her as my mother,
notwithstanding that I am not worthy   25,376
that a lady so holy and good
be given to me and placed in my keeping.
O master, when I consider
your situation and what I see,   25,380
I am shocked.
I cannot be shocked enough,
when those false and evil Jews
full of envy   25,384
want to take away your life today
without your having deserved death,
for which your mother
feels such bitter distress   25,388
that there is no heart that knows it
without feeling affliction.
It still seems bold
that to give her comfort   25,392
you chose me,
who am so troubled by sorrow
that I do not know where

25,357 John 19:26, "Woman, behold thy son." See also *Passion d'Arras* (lines 17,032–33).
25,363 John 19:27 and *Passion d'Arras* (l. 17,035).

I can direct myself.   25,396
Do you think then that I can sufficiently
provide comfort
for her terrible pains,
seeing their number, and   25,400
when I do not know which of us two
must suffer more?
One must seek comfort
from him who can help   25,404
and give joy.
But, as for me, I am unable,
for the greatest part of my good
I lose on this day.   25,408
O noble lady of excellence,
most holy and precious flower,
blessed body,
you hear what my master has said.   25,412
He has willed to elect you
my mother through his decree.
OUR LADY John, I do not want to oppose it,
even though I make a very pitiful exchange   25,416
today, when I exchange °
for my perfect, natural son
a new adopted son;
for God, a simple, transient man;   25,420
for the Lord, the servant;
and for the master, the disciple.
My sad and miserable countenance
suppresses its troubles;   25,424
My will conforms completely
to the divine will.
Let it befall my son in the manner
his father has prepared.   25,428
MAGDALENE O lady adorned with virtue
and the most constant among all,
your response is so pleasing
that every heart is relieved.   25,432
PHARES Jesus, you daydream too much
and are greatly reproached
for staying so long

25,417–22 Mary also complains of exchanging her natural son for an adopted one
and the master for the disciple in the *Passion Isabeau* (lines 3,941–61).

on this cross that is so disparaged. 25,436
Why did you not just now invoke
God's aid in your misery?
Since you say he is your father,
he will help you without fail. 25,440
EMILIUS Believe me, if he could have come down,
he wouldn't have waited so long.
GRIFFON I stretched him out so well
that he can't remove himself. 25,444
JEROBOAM Come on, Jesus, do your duty, °
speed up the business; it's not fast enough.
If you are the king of Israel,
quickly descend from this high cross, 25,448
and we'll believe in you without fail.
Now, get to work on this problem right away.
ORILLART Speak loudly. He doesn't hear you.
He's thinking about his worries. 25,452
MARDOCEE Now we see his folly
and the venom which he cherished.
He saved others all right,
but he remains here in the mire. 25,456
GESTAS Jesus, it seems strange to me
since you revived the dead,
that your force does not liberate us.
If you were able to do this, 25,460
you are really horrible and mean
for not liberating us.
But you have neither strength nor power
and are a poor man, so I believe. 25,464
Ah, villainous and accursed cross,
must I end my days on you?
Ah, isn't there any comfort or help
which can give me respite from death? 25,468
I don't care where it might come from,
whether from false tricks or true,
from God or all the devils,
as long as I could escape from death! 25,472
BRAYART Companions, after the games and amusements,
I would gladly know
what we will do with the clothing
of Jesus and his cohorts. 25,476

25,445–50 From Matthew 27:42–43 and Mark 15:32.

GRIFFON Neither debating nor gambling are necessary.
    By rights, it's all mine.
CLAQUEDENT Oh yeah, why?
GRIFFON On the grounds
    that I executed them.   25,480
    It is the custom in all cities
    that the executioner gets the spoils.
BROYEFORT Do you know what? Let nothing divide us.
    No matter how it goes with the thieves,   25,484
    we'll have our share of
    Jesus' garments, which will be drawn by lottery.
ORILLART It's only fair that all be divided.
    Each one of us has a right.   25,488
    If you hanged them, fine;
    we also certainly helped you.
CLAQUEDENT By rights, whoever holds the foot
    gets as much as the one who flays.   25,492
GRIFFON Must it be so?
BRAYART It has to be so.
    He's an idiot who doesn't believe it.
GRIFFON Since we must steer through this difficulty,
    let us briefly consider, without arguing,   25,496
    how many men we are to split the reward.
ORILLART We are four all together. °
BROYEFORT It seems to me there are five.
    My lords, count at your leisure.   25,500
GRIFFON You aren't one, by your leave.
    Your muzzle droops a little too sadly.
BROYEFORT I'll have at least a piece,
    if there's either goodness or honor in you.   25,504
    I served you every day;
    what will I get for all my pains?
CLAQUEDENT You'll have the bloody plague
    to wrap around you instead of a cape.   25,508
BROYEFORT Take it! If this deal escapes you,
    you won't have any as good this month.
BRAYART Did I divide it correctly?
    Here are four parts divided   25,512
    and so exactly arranged
    that one cannot take away or add anything.

25,498 John 19:23 mentions four soldiers. In Gréban, they are Roman. In Marcadé, they are four Jews.

GRIFFON This is for me.

ORILLART Bravo for the master!
    He certainly knows how to take the best!   25,516

BRAYART And this for me.

CLAQUEDENT What a leader!
    Since each takes his own,
    I'll take this.

ORILLART And here's mine.
    I won't lose everything today.   25,520
    To finish this up right away
    while we're all ready,
    let's next share this one,
    so that each one has his piece.   25,524

GRIFFON It's not wise to cut it,
    seeing that it's of a strange structure,
    all one piece without a seam. °
    Let's play a game of chance   25,528
    to decide who'll have it.

ORILLART I agree completely
    without opposing you in anything.
    We must figure out
    what kind of game we'll play. °   25,532
    Let's draw lots.

BRAYART Come on, let's draw.
    Whoever has the longest, takes it.

CLAQUEDENT That game is not at all to my liking,
    because of all the cheating in it.   25,536

BRAYART Well then, think of another
    that's a little more fun.
    Griffon, you've seen a lot of them
    and know more than ten games.   25,540
    If you know any, tell us,
    and we'll follow your decision.

GRIFFON Our course of action will be such
    as you will hear me describe.   25,544
    I must return to the city
    for a short time since I hope

25,527 Only John 19:23 mentions that the garment is seamless.

25,532 Matthew 27:35, Mark 15:24, Luke 23:34, and John 19:24 all describe the casting of lots for Christ's garment. Satan's introduction and explanation of dice occurs in the *Passion d'Arras* (lines 16,360–416). In *Le Mystère de la Passion de Nostre Seigneur* (128) the soldiers also use dice.

to find a huge axe
with which I'll cut the necks   25,548
of these thieves in order to
break their knees before sunset.
Think quickly of some game
and while going to the city,   25,552
I'll also think about
finding some diversion.
ORILLART No one among us disagrees.
Go and return quickly.   25,556
SATAN I must change rapidly
and alter my face a little,
so I can work out some malice
against that scoundrel who is going away.   25,560
If the devil doesn't carry him off,
I'll soon attack him.
Poor man of feeble nature,
where do you wish to go?   25,564
GRIFFON To a place where I have something to do.
Let me go my way.
SATAN Stop, stop my friend.
I want to say two words to you.   25,568
I know what your intention is
and what you are grumbling about.
GRIFFON Oh you do, do you?
SATAN I'll tell you this much:
you're breaking your head   25,572
to find some game of chance
which you can play so well
that you can win
a miserable and quite wretched garment   25,576
that belonged to Jesus.
GRIFFON You're right.
I don't know who revealed it to you.
SATAN Nothing can be hidden from me.
I was able to perceive it.   25,580
If you want to know a good game,
I'll teach you an appropriate one
by which you will not fail
to win this robe on the spot.   25,584
No cheating or trickery
can ever do you wrong.
GRIFFON You surprise me with your proposition.
I have no belief or faith in it.   25,588

SATAN I'll tell you one more time
    that when you learn this excellent game
    and play it according to my instructions,
    you will not fail to come away with   25,592
    the robe.
GRIFFON Well then, I ask you
    to show me how it's played.
SATAN It's clear and easy enough.
    Look with your greedy eyes.   25,596
    Do you see this small piece of bone
    with six square sides?
    As soon as I've gotten it ready,
    you will surely understand and say that indeed   25,600
    a better game was never made.
    Look. You see that it's cut at right angles?
    First, on this square put
    a point so that it appears   25,604
    in the name of God the father;
    two will be placed on this one
    in contempt of the father and the son;
    then you find three on this side   25,608
    in contempt of the trinity;
    four will have their places here
    to spite the evangelists
    who will write about God's law;   25,612
    on this other side will be
    five well-placed points to spite
    the five wounds of Christ,
    which you see on the cross there.   25,616
GRIFFON For the five wounds? How so?
    You show that you have not seen him.
    There are more than ten thousand wounds;
    you reduce them to too few in number.   25,620
SATAN I speak to you of the principle ones
    piercing Jesus' body.
GRIFFON Therefore, you lie as before
    because if you speak to me of the large ones,   25,624
    only four were given;
    I've looked closely at each one.
SATAN Soon there will be another one,
    which will make the fifth.   25,628
    Let it suffice you that it will be thus,
    to spite the five said wounds.
    As many times as you say these words,

you'll roll that number of points.   25,632
GRIFFON Here is another square.
          How many more points are necessary?
SATAN Six points and no more,
          and it's the highest number,   25,636
          undoubtedly marked
          to spite in deed and words
          the whole court of paradise.
          I can't preach anymore about it,   25,640
          and yet I want to tell you
          that you cannot find under the heavens
          a game more useful to you
          for winning.   25,644
GRIFFON I certainly think not.
          Good sir, tell me the name
          of this beautiful, newly invented game.
SATAN You must call it a die,
          a name of great nobility.   25,648
GRIFFON And if someone inquires after the inventor
          what shall I say?
SATAN Without telling tales,
          you will say that the devil made it.
          You will not incur a lie.   25,652
          And whenever you play,
          either you or someone in your place,
          and the result is not to your liking,
          if you need one point, think   25,656
          and say, "Roll in hatred for the father."
          If two have been badly thrown together,
          say here: "Roll in contempt of the son
          and the father together."   25,660
          And so on in this manner
          as I showed you before.
          If at this point you direct yourself
          to whomever you wish to shame,   25,664
          you will not fail to win
          as much money as comes forth.
GRIFFON I'll do my very best
          to spite and deny.   25,668
          To get things going as fast as possible
          we'll part here, friend.
          I'll return to my companions
          to teach them this game.   25,672
SATAN They will play so gladly

that no one will be able to quit.

GRIFFON Friends, would you like to know
    a very nice and pleasant game?   25,676

ORILLART Come on, let's see it.
    We were not expecting anything less.

GRIFFON This is exactly our kettle of fish.
    Look at this device here.   25,680

CLAQUEDENT Where the devil did you find this?
    Griffon, I'm really surprised.

BRAYART I've never seen anything like it,
    nor do I remember such a great game.   25,684

GRIFFON Don't worry about where it comes from.
    Let's take Jesus' robe
    and throw this die for it;
    and then whoever can, will win it.   25,688

ORILLART You must therefore teach us
    the game, how it's played.

GRIFFON Whoever has the most points wins.
    I don't see any other way.   25,692
    And if two roll the same number,
    they must roll again.

CLAQUEDENT The game seems very good.
    I'll enjoy it only too gladly.   25,696
    Who'll start first?
    Let him make haste, the time is right.

GRIFFON It can't matter; it's all the same.
    Whoever has the die, rolls it by chance.   25,700

BRAYART Here begins the match,
    since no one opposes me.
    Argh, I rolled only a one.
    May this be in contempt of God!   25,704

GRIFFON How are you already such a good master
    without your having been taught?

ORILLART I hardly rolled any higher.
    I have a two; my part is done.   25,708
    Cursed be the false prophet
    whom I see crucified there!

CLAQUEDENT I rolled a little higher.
    I have a three for all my pains.   25,712
    May the whole sovereign court
    be cursed and disgraced!

GRIFFON Let me roll. Make room
    so that I can get ready.   25,716
    There it is. There's six.

There need be no more discussion.
This robe is mine.
BRAYART It is so.
May the devil break his paw!   25,720
Have we lost it so quickly
through your chatter and tricks?
The false game that you explained to us,
cursed be the one who created it.   25,724
ORILLART Yes, and the one who taught it to us.
Losing troubles my heart greatly.
GRIFFON I don't care, let everyone be cursed
since I hold the best part.   25,728
You'll never see it again;
it goes with me.
PILATE My lords, I see great marvels.
I have not understood these things.   25,732
The day has ended very early.
We can hardly see anything on earth. °
CENTURION My heart is in my throat
because of the fear spreading in me.   25,736
Look how late it seems
and how darkness abounds,
and it is not yet noon.
The sky must be off-track.   25,740
ANNAS My lords, if God is to give you joy,
you must not ever talk so.
Did you never see
a solar eclipse? Understand that   25,744
this is what you see.
You must not be frightened of it.
RUBION If the world should end
without ever having a future,   25,748
it would be a very dark,
very terrible and frightening time.
ASCANIUS It's still getting darker.
There's not a heart that doesn't still tremble.   25,752
JESUS *quartum verbum*
Deus meus, Deus meus, °
ut quid dereliquisti me?

25,734 Matthew 27:45; Mark 15:33; Luke 23:44.
25,754–55 Matthew 27:46–47 and Mark 15:34, "My God, my God, why hast thou forsaken me?"

My God, my Father from on high,
you who see all that you have formed, 25,756
look at your son who is punished most severely,
who has committed no wrong or foolishness.
Hely, lama zabathani. °
God, why have you forgotten me? 25,760
BROYEFORT Listen, lords, he called
Elijah, one of your prophets.
Because of this, watch what you do.
If he comes, he will deliver him. 25,764
ISACAR See if he will come.
We must all listen.
JORAN I think he'll wait in vain.
He's a long way from being rescued. 25,768
JACOB If he calls Elijah to descend, °
I think he'll wait in vain.
JOATHAN Elijah could well give him
freedom, if there is recourse to him. 25,772
ISACAR I think he'll wait in vain.
He's a long way from being rescued.
It will be three days
before we observe his end. 25,776
JESUS *quintum verbum* Delightful human nature
my dearest and most beloved race,
scitio, I have a fierce thirst °
for restoring your heritage. 25,780
I have martyred my flesh for you
as much as it can withstand.
Only the tongue remains,
whose strength will not diminish. 25,784
RUBION This Jesus begins to give up.
He complains of the thirst he has.
SALMANASAR I'll take care of that, °
and since I have it in mind, 25,788
I'll soon give him to drink,
enough to quench his thirst.
Here's a rich and expensive beverage

25,759 *Hely lama zabathani.* In the *Passion d'Arras* (l. 17,262) the same quotation is
used.
25,769 Matthew 27:47; Mark 15:35.
25,779 John 19:28, "I thirst." See also *Passion d'Arras* (l. 17,299).
25,787–822 John 19:29 and *Passion d'Arras* (lines 17,300–318).

to fatten up a skinny man;   25,792
it's of gall and vinegar
with myrrh mixed in it.
PHARES You speak well; you're my friend.
But how will you give it to him?   25,796
SALMANASAR Easy! Here I've soaked
a sponge with bitter hyssop;
I must attach it
to a good, straight, long reed   25,800
to administer it to him; thus,
he won't risk getting drunk.
JORAM Come on, get to it right away;
this is the work of a good man.   25,804
SALMANASAR Take it, prophet, take it.
Drink this excellently prepared wine.
It's not mulled wine or claret.
It's beverage of another kind.   25,808

[*He puts a sponge at the end of a lance and puts it
against Jesus' mouth. Jesus pulls his mouth away.*]

NENBROTH He throws his head back;
he tried a little,
but as soon as he tasted it,
he realized it's not what he asked for.   25,812
ASCANIUS His palate is too refined.
He would have liked better a glass
of wine and a piece of bread
to sink his teeth into.   25,816
SALMANASAR I'm pushing it inside by force,
but he resists it as much as he can.
RABANUS He has enough misfortune.
Since this drink doesn't please him,   25,820
leave him there as he is.
It's enough that he tried it.
CENTURION Everyone must really be afraid
of looking at the sun in the sky.   25,824
I do not know if the atmosphere is natural,
but the darkness frightens me.
JESUS *sextum verbum*
Consummatum est. It is finished. °

25,827 John 19:30, "It is finished." Marcadé's *Passion d'Arras* (l. 17,322) also
preserves the Latin here.

All the scriptures
that man ever wrote about me 25,828
are at this hour fulfilled.
Now is terminated
the mystery of the passion 25,832
whose goal has been determined
by human redemption.
OUR LADY O painful separation,
the most piteous of sorrows! 25,836
O terrible and contemptuous Death,
look at my languor;
I entreat you, and you flee from me.
Death, how can you allow 25,840
my heart to feel such distress
without abating and reducing it?
My child, my offspring, my son,
alas, you go off to death! 25,844
Alas, do not leave me,
who must be guided by you alone.
It is enough for me to die with you.
I will receive only good when I die; 25,848
living here without you
will be an even harder death for me.
MAGDALENE His whole body endures such pain
that it can take no more without giving up its soul. 25,852
Devout lady, console yourself a little
over your piteous situation.
JESUS *septimum verbum*
O Pater, in manus tuas °
commendo spiritum meum. 25,856
For the power which you have,
my father, and by your worthy name,
I will have no more days after this one.
I part from the worldly realm 25,860
and in parting with a piteous cry,
I place my soul into your hands.

25,855–56 Luke 23:46, "Father, into thy hands I commend my spirit." See also
Passion d'Arras (l. 17,332).
after 25,862 The stage directions correspond to Matthew 27:51.

Here Jesus bows his head and gives up his soul.
The earth must tremble. The veil of the temple must split in two,
and the rocks must break in two °

SATAN Here is such a sudden development
　　　that I don't have a hold   25,864
　　　on this Jesus, who amazes me.
　　　He's dead, his end has come.
　　　But I don't know
　　　what has become of his soul or to what place   25,868
　　　it goes or in what direction.
　　　But I have a great fear
　　　that he is moving toward our manor
　　　to break the doors and bolts   25,872
　　　and to destroy us and plunder everything.
　　　I fear that he is already near
　　　and because of this, I will run after him
　　　to arrive before him if I can.   25,876

Here he goes to Hell

CENTURION In my heart I marvel °
　　　at this man, who in dying
　　　let out such a great cry,
　　　considering the weakness of his body.   25,880
RUBION I don't ever remember
　　　hearing such a strong human voice.
OUR LADY O my son, my hard and unpleasant life
　　　distresses me too much.   25,884
　　　Where are you?

Here she falls fainting under the cross

MAGDALENE There she is, passed out,
　　　fallen in a faint on the ground.
GRIFFON There's not a heart that is not gripped by pity
　　　on seeing this unfortunate woman   25,888
　　　who remains on the ground,
　　　having fainted in grief.
ORILLART Let's carry her to the rear with us,
　　　so that we no longer have to hear such a racket.   25,892

25,877–80 Roy (233) sees the Centurion's remark as having its source in Nicholas
of Lyra, who explains that Christ's great cry could not have been made through
natural strength. The Centurion in Marcadé makes no similar comment, but his
counterpart does so in the *Passion Isabeau* (lines 4,241–44).

Get away from here, filthy group!
You can't stay so close.
If you want to see your master,
you'll have to look at him from afar. 25,896

Here they carry Our Lady away

PILATE Centurion, would you watch over
these scoundrels for a time.
I'm leaving this place
because the great signs that I see 25,900
astound both my senses and my voice,
so that I can hardly say a word.
CENTURION I will gladly do it sir.
Nothing will impede my duty. 25,904

Here Pilate leaves with his people

RUBION I think that the world will disappear.
Such events were never before seen.
The earth trembles up and down,
so that all men are frightened. 25,908
Stones split in half,
so that nothing remains whole.
ASCANIUS Fleeing would have been a smart idea
or hiding in the mountains. 25,912
Never have more horrible signs
been shown on earth.
Intense darkness has come about,
even more profound than before. 25,916
EMILIUS Walk forth from here
to see amazing things.
You will see many tombs
completely open, I guarantee you. 25,920
But what this signifies to us
no one can say.
CENTURION The truth can no longer be hidden.
Whoever has no belief is foolish. 25,924
Jesus' action is so manifest
that it frightens and wounds us all.
He did not deserve the anguish
he endured in this place. 25,928
As a result I confess in truth °

25,929–30 Matthew 27:54; Mark 15:39; *Passion d'Arras* (lines 17,357–58).

that he was the true son of God.

SAINT DENIS OF ATHENS   Lords, the good craftswoman Nature °
was never seen to deviate in such a manner   25,932
from the normal course
as we see today.
You all know that no one
but Jupiter, the sovereign god,   25,936
seated on the royal throne,
has governed the firmament
for a long time and so very correctly,
that in his noble monarchy   25,940
never was a mistake seen.
Everything is done very regularly.
Never was an error found
nor did anything abandon its order   25,944
for astronomy to criticize
or find any defect.
Our worthy Aristotle,
who certainly had knowledge,   25,948
says in the second book of Physics °
on this point, "If we examine
all the time that we have known
since the time of the reliable philosophers,   25,952
our most ancient predecessors,
and if we have well retained that
which we and they have known,
we do not find through any observation whatsoever,   25,956
that anything in the heavens is caused by chance."
And as if he wanted to prove
that one could not find a mistake,
there never was any flaw except for this one,   25,960
which is so obvious and evident;
such an error has never happened.
This eclipse is unnatural,
indeed, and so powerfully against nature   25,964

25,931 The story of Dionysius of Athens or Dionysius the Areopagite is found in
the *Passion d'Arras* (lines 17,190–261) and in *The Golden Legend* entry for October
9. Gréban replaces Dionysius' companion, Apolliphanus, with Empedocles and
omits the building of the altar to the unknown God. Empedocles, a Greek
philosopher and statesman (490–430 B.C.E.), is noted for his theory of the four
elements: earth, water, air, and fire.

25,949 Aristotle (*Physics*, 2.3 [196b]) writes that nothing happens in the heavens by
chance.

that there is no wise creature
who could explain it by reason.

EMPEDOCLES Your speech is based on good reasoning,
    Denis, our most wise teacher.   25,968
    In our time there never occurred
    what is happening at this hour.
    What do you think of it?

SAINT DENIS It is necessary
    and inevitable to conclude   25,972
    that the moon goes against nature
    and has changed to a new course,
    because for fourteen days it
    has been sitting in opposition   25,976
    to the house of the sun.
    Now it has stirred from its place
    and at the right spot interposes
    between the earth and the sun,   25,980
    which due to its unusual conduct
    causes this eclipse.

EMPEDOCLES What do you figure from this,
    master, I entreat you,   25,984
    for we are so depressed
    that we can stand no more.

SAINT DENIS As for me, I say and conclude that
    it must be that the prime mover,   25,988
    god and governor of the earth,
    permits it by some mischance
    or that the whole structure
    of the world as it is constructed   25,992
    will be quickly dissolved and destroyed.
    I do not see any other cause.

EMPEDOCLES The argument is good and forceful
    and probably provides the reason.   25,996

Silete

GOD Now has my dear, worthy son
    passed the agonizing step
    of death in misery and anguish
    through a pitiful execution.   26,000
    Angels, cry out in lamentation
    and bear very piteous looks
    for the death of your good king,
    who suffered such testing,   26,004
    offering his precious body

to the painful passion.
Lament his cruel death,
do not cease to mourn him,   26,008
but consider Isaiah,
who pronounced these words about you
when saying: *angeli pacis*
dolentes amare flebunt. °   26,012
All those who were and are to come
will not be able to restrain themselves
from lamenting and grieving over his death.
All nature gives way to it,   26,016
all nature feels his death
and experiences sadness and grief
for the death of its creator.
I know that you feel thus.   26,020
I want you to sing a tearful melody
as your only consolation.

> *Here the angels sing one or two verses of*
> *the Kyrie eleison from Tenebrae; then Raphael says*

RAPHAEL City of Zion,
cease all exultation   26,024
and joy;
With desolation
and confusion
replace your gaiety.   26,028
When your king leaves you,
your crown ceases,
your good departs;
you lose your nobility,   26,032
you lose your wealth,
you no longer have a share.
URIEL Beautiful Jerusalem,
solemn city,   26,036
what evil have you done?
Cruel serpent,
stinging and fatal,
acknowledge your action,   26,040
how you have done wrong

26,011 *angeli pacis dolentes amare flebunt.* Isaiah 33:7, "The angels of peace shall weep bitterly." The Latin quotation is also found in the *Passion Isabeau* (line 4,650).

in destroying today
your Christ, your savior!
Bewail your misdeed,   26,044
vile and hypocritical;
know your sin.
MICHAEL O noble Judea,
nobly founded   26,048
and of great antiquity,
you were once pure.
Now you have poorly upheld
your nobility   26,052
when out of cruelty
you have expelled
your loyal pastor.
For its own good,   22,056
noble Creator,
avenge such severity!
GABRIEL O sweet Virgin,
more worthy than the others,   26,060
take comfort.
If the wicked race
has destroyed
your dear comfort,   26,064
remember
that, his costly death
is so highly profitable
that without this noble support   26,068
man would not enjoy
everlasting glory.
OUR LADY Gabriel, my faithful guardian,
even though this death is dearly paid for,   26,072
the will of God my father
and his noble desires are fulfilled,
for I have in me the firm hope
that my son will not leave me,   26,076
but on the third day will rise
and will return from death to life.
This is my belief. My soul is enraptured with it.
No one could separate me from it.   26,080
SATAN It took me no time to return °

26,081–194 The Harrowing of Hell occurs in the Fourth Day in the *Passion d'Arras*
(lines 20,529–21,145).

to the infernal abyss.
Lucifer, listen to what I say.
We must fortify our doors. 26,084
Here is Jesus' soul coming
to plunder us, a hundred against one.
LUCIFER Come on, devils, horrible community,
close your doors and make them strong, 26,088
put in many bolts, °
stack up more than a thousand rods,
and make sure you don't fall asleep.
Soon you will see our adversary. 26,092
CERBERUS King Lucifer, let me do this.
In spite of the strength he can show,
I will stop his entry completely.
I have armed our gate 26,096
with great boulders of metal
as large as huge castles
and have put more than a thousand iron bars
all across the opening. 26,100
FERGALUS To be safe, put there also
this huge fixed bolt right away.
ASTAROTH Let's risk all against everything,
condemned devils; it's time. 26,104
We must work at it,
for if he enters at his demand,
we will suffer the greatest loss
that could ever come upon us. 26,108
CERBERUS Now let him come boldly.
Unless he overcomes every devil,
he will not break the door.
There are many defenses. 26,112
JESUS' SPIRIT *Attollite portas* °
principes vestras et elevamini porte eternales etc.

and the souls respond:

Quis est iste rex glorie?
JESUS' SPIRIT *Dominus fortis et potens, dominus potens in prelio.*
Attolite portas principes, etc.

26,089 The command to bar the doors is found in the *Gospel of Nicodemus.*
after 26,112 The *Gospel of Nicodemus*, Chap. 21, "Lift up your gates, O rulers, and
be lifted up, O everlasting doors, and the King of glory shall come in. Who is this
King of glory?" See also Psalm 23:7–10.

and they respond:

Quis est iste rex glorie?
JESUS' SPIRIT *Deus virtutum ipse rex glorie. Attollite portas principes, etc.*

Here the doors must fall when Jesus strikes them with his cross,
and then Jesus' spirit says again

False devil, deprived of glory,
you strive against me
and fortify your doors against me for nothing.   26,116
You derive confusion from it,
and I have obtained victory.
For a long time you have held
the human race captive;   26,120
through me they will be released
in spite of you, without their being prevented.
The price was paid by me dearly enough.
I endured cruel death,   26,124
through which strength is given to me
to pillage your possessions
and rob and despoil you of
the good inhabitants whom you hold.   26,128
They are mine—they will no longer be yours.
You elevated yourself over them,
and you will be subjugated without cease
to this powerful and worthy cross,   26,132
to this high and terrible sign
which I now possess.
By the cross you will be deprived
of all the power and strength   26,136
with which you were too much invested
and will be defrauded of all your false tricks.
THE DEVILS *together* Alas, alas, alas, alas,
here is a terrible punishment!   26,140
JESUS' SPIRIT *takes Adam by the hand and says*
Adam, friend, peace be with you
and all your just and good sons!
In these dark prisons
you have lamented a long time.   26,144
I will lead you to another place
where you will obtain solace,
and there you will all wait for me
until I rise to heaven.   26,148
Then I will transport you

to my everlasting realm.

ADAM O noble, pleasing succor,
    price of dear redemption,   26,152
    sovereign, charitable comfort,
    noble atonement,
    O deep compassion,
    too full of loving mercy for mankind,   26,156
    blessed be the Passion
    by which we are redeemed!

SAINT JOHN THE BAPTIST O sovereign mediator
    between God and human nature,   26,160
    once I was the herald
    of your sovereign coming.
    My words were not empty
    when I called you the *agnus Dei*, °   26,164
    for by your goodness filled with love,
    tu tollis peccata mundi. °

EVE Blessed be the worthy servant
    and the God-favored womb   26,168
    of the blessed maid
    who carried such worthy fruit!
    We see his divinity,
    the one who delivers us from servitude.   26,172
    But through her, have we been presented today
    with the noble goodness that liberates us.

DAVID O succor from the pure deity,
    we have waited a long time for you   26,176
    and have called for you with cautious care
    as the gift promised by God!
    We have waited so long,
    covered in much affliction   26,180
    until you descended
    to our extraordinary joy.

ISAIAH Now nothing hurts us
    since we see the presence   26,184
    of the noble magnificence
    which leads us to his glory.

EZEKIEL All our grievous sorrow is gone,
    and we have joy in abundance   26,188
    in contemplating the divine essence,

26,164 John 1:29, "Lamb of God."
26,166 John 1:29, "you take away the sins of the world."

the sight of which rejoices every good heart.

JEREMIAH Blessed be he who directed us
    to this path for our offenses!   26,192
    Sweet Jesus' divine providence
    leads us.

Here Jesus leads them to a certain place and,
in the meantime, a great tempest is made in Hell, and then

LUCIFER *says*
    Devils, I'm enraged, I'm drowning.
    I'm burning like a red furnace.   26,196
    I'm going crazy. I'm convulsed
    by the anger wringing me.
CERBERUS We are wronged, we are wronged,
    and because of this robbery,   26,200
    I appeal to the great judgment,
    because the false Jesus has no right here.
LUCIFER Your appeal will accomplish nothing.
    Jesus, who did it,   26,204
    will be the judge and the adversary.
    But to regain what he steals from us
    run all of you after him;
    thus, you can recover the prey.   26,208
ASTAROTH In a lost match there is no race.
    We are here so beaten
    and so weakened by rage
    that it's useless to run.   26,212
CERBERUS Argh, what great deviltry
    and what immeasurable rage!
    Now in despair is
    the well of Tartarus. °   26,216
LUCIFER What kind of grimace are you making Cerberus?
    What the devil are you brooding about?
    Is all lost? What's going on?
    Did he plunder everything from everywhere?   26,220
CERBERUS No, may the devil take it,
    there still remain an abundance
    of damned in our house,
    down there, at the bottom of hell;   26,224

26,216 *la fountaine de Tartarus.* In Greek mythology, Tartarus was the lower
division of the underworld, also known as the prison of the Sons of Earth
(Hamilton, 39).

but he robbed us
of too much at one time,
for he carried off the most select
and the flower of our inheritance.   26,228
LUCIFER Ah, spark of hateful fury
contained in a vile substance,
fatal and venomous beverage,
putrid poison, death unleashed!   26,232
Death, Death, where are you shut up?
Daughter engendered by me,
glance at the sorrow I feel;
I seek you everywhere, and you escape me.   26,236
Come here, Satan.
SATAN I cannot.
That loud cry is not worthy of you.
I'm dead or nearly so
and will not stir either head or foot.   26,240
LUCIFER Rotten dragon, stinking beast,
hideous serpent, old crocodile,
your stinking and vile substance
will not die so quietly.   26,244
Come quickly.
SATAN I cannot do otherwise.
Even so, I'm moving too quickly.
LUCIFER Why?
SATAN I'm limping on one paw.
I can barely move.   26,248
Alas!
LUCIFER Fergalus, is he telling the truth?
Is he limping so badly that he howls?
FERGALUS No, but he fakes it
so very well that it's a great pity.   26,252
BERICH He's a false, hypocritical thief;
he'll pay for this,
for it's through him that our prey
is so miserably lost.   26,256
LUCIFER Are you telling me the truth?
SATAN The scoundrel lies
by the false heart of his guts,
and if I have any wickedness left,   26,260
I'll call him to the field of battle,
for I did my best
through artful and false means
to protect the infernal rights   26,264

over all the devils of the house.

LUCIFER Let's leave off this fatal despair
　　　which drowns my heart with rage.
　　　The more we speak of it, the more I worry.　　26,268
　　　What's lost is lost,
　　　but let's all think of those remaining,
　　　to save them as best we can.

BERICH That's a good idea.　　26,272

LUCIFER Now we'll see
　　　who will perform the best mission.
　　　Satan, take a trip
　　　and bring me, if you believe in me,
　　　those two thieves on the cross;
　　　they cannot live long.　　26,276

SATAN If I don't immediately deliver both of them
　　　to you, bound and chained,
　　　I'll let you beat me
　　　through all the infernal chambers.　　26,280

LUCIFER Now go then! May all the black devils
　　　of the horrible desolate place
　　　bring you back scorched or burned!

JEROBOAM Lords of Judea's law,　　26,284
　　　having watched over the business
　　　of the execution
　　　of Jesus and his Passion,
　　　you can see very great signs　　26,288
　　　appearing at the time of his death
　　　at which everyone may be frightened
　　　and which make my whole heart tremble.
　　　In short, I don't know what to say of this　　26,292
　　　except that I dread and fear
　　　that in the end a great evil will come upon us.
　　　But no matter what happens,
　　　because he is dying on the cross,　　26,296
　　　one must see to the rest of the matter
　　　in order to dispose of it, if possible.

CAIAPHAS Speak, and we will listen.
　　　Jeroboam, explain the situation.　　26,300

JEROBOAM I take into consideration, sir Caiaphas,
　　　that by annual custom it is now
　　　our very solemn feast
　　　of Passover which we observe strictly.　　26,304
　　　It's my opinion that it's not good
　　　for us, being pastors,

that the bodies of these evildoers
remain hanging on the cross   26,308
this sabbath.
CAIAPHAS Let them be taken down!
In short, you speak wisely,
but we must have permission   26,312
from Pilate our procurator,
and may he speed up
their death if they have not expired.
ANNAS That's a good point. Now come.   26,316
We're still making progress.

Here the Pharisees come to Pilate

CAIAPHAS Sir procurator, may the high mover,
governing and guiding the beautiful heavens,
send you comfort and aid   26,320
and increase your honor.
PILATE What do my good lords who
come here to our palace request?
CAIAPHAS Sir procurator, the case is as follows; °
you know that by our demand   26,324
three people of dishonest lives
have been put on the cross to die.
We have come to ask you,
in order to avoid greater harm,   26,328
if you would mind speeding up their death,
for they have languished long
in great torment on their crosses.
Their pain must be sufficient enough.   26,332
Also, you know, dear sir,
that it is our Sabbath and holiday
which everyone observes and celebrates
excellently in devotion.   26,336
Thus, it would be a great shame to see
their bodies fixed there this whole day.
For this reason, without further delay,
have their knees broken,   26,340
so that they die immediately,
and then they will be removed.
PILATE Dearest lords, your entreaty
is my command. Realize   26,344

26,323–42 John 19:31; *Passion d'Arras* (lines 17,451–64).

that I feel enough displeasure
over the affair of Jesus the prophet
and over a sentence having ever been passed.
I depart very worried,   26,348
but always confident
that you will be my aides,
true friends and good protectors,
if any grief comes to me for this deed.   26,352
O affliction, I did what I did
and am content that it remain so.
ANNAS Sir governor, I assure you
it will not last another day;   26,356
and when the affair is over,
and when some take his side
or want to avenge his death,
you and we, with common purpose,   26,360
will unite and be as one
in defending ourselves against all comers.
PILATE That is well said. Come here, officers.
You will perform a small service.   26,364
Go to the place of execution
with axes and knives
and dismember the thieves,
as you know the custom is.   26,368
BRAYART And what about Jesus?
PILATE You're not very smart!
Listen to this churl!
You will finish him off too.
This villain doesn't understand a thing.   26,372
BRAYART Now you speak more clearly.
Whoever doesn't know, asks.
If there were thirty-seven of them,
I would dispose of them straightaway.   26,376
PILATE Come on, comrades, walk, walk.
Go keep him company.
ORILLART Me too!
CLAQUEDENT I wouldn't miss this.   26,380
I'll bring my huge axe.
GRIFFON Let's follow, then.
BROYEFORT Truly, may God help me,
it'll be really worthwhile.

LONGINUS My lords, passing through here, °
 where are you going at this hour?   26,384
BROYEFORT Sir Longinus, may God help you!
 What are you doing now?
 We're going to mount Calvary.
 to speed up Jesus' death.   26,388
 If you would like to go there,
 we'll provide you good company.
LONGINUS Ah, my lords, as you know
 I haven't been able to see for a long time. 26,392
BRAYART Don't worry. We'll guide you well;
 the road is very good and wide.
LONGINUS Would you take the trouble to do that?
 If I thought I wouldn't hinder you,   26,396
 I would gladly go
 with the lance I bear.
BRAYART The journey will not trouble you.
 If you please, walk forward.   26,400
 I'll take it upon myself to lead you
 and bring you back if necessary.
LONGINUS Are you asking if it pleases me?
 Very much, I tell you.   26,404
BROYEFORT Let's be on our way.
LONGINUS I agree
 because for a long time I've had the desire
 to do harm to Jesus,
 and if you give me permission,   26,408
 I will wound him again
 no matter what the consequences are.
CLAQUEDENT One cannot punish him enough.
 They want him to be handed over
 to everyone in general   26,412
 as a condemned evildoer.
DYMAS Alas, I experience great suffering
 and a lasting, severe pain.   26,416
 My life lasts too long
 in this terrible misery.
 I ask for bitter Death,

26,383–410; 26,491–520; 26,543–63 The story of Longinus is told in *The Gospel of Nicodemus* and in *The Golden Legend*. In the *Passion d'Arras* (lines 17,739–892), Annas orders Longinus to wound Christ. In Gréban, Longinus acts of his own will, motivated by his hatred for Christ.

who does not want to listen to my complaints.   26,420

GESTAS I feel pain that is so hard to bear
    that I can neither live nor die.

BRAYART You will soon be freed of it. °
    Rejoice freely,   26,424
    here is your last sacrament
    fully prepared at this hour.

ORILLART Deal him a forceful blow,
    bringing him to his last moment.   26,428

BRAYART Very well. Don't worry about it.
    He'll get more than ten of them.

GRIFFON And in the meantime I'll get rid of
    this other scoundrel here.   26,432

BRAYART Come here, rascal, come here.
    You won't have one good bone in your thighs
    that's not broken, not if I can help it.
    Here is my weapon, all ready.   26,436

DYMAS Praised be God, since it pleases him
    to lead me to this lot!
    It is not God who causes me misfortune
    but my bad conduct.   26,440
    I die by just judgment.
    I have truly deserved death.
    Jesus, sweet fruit of life,
    who promised me paradise,
    at this difficult parting,
    I entrust my soul to your keeping.

BRAYART You won't ever chatter again.
    You won't have a leg that I don't crush.   26,448

CLAQUEDENT He certainly reaps bitter fruit. °
    Buy some if you like.
    Blood flows from all sides
    down to the mountain top.   26,452

GRIFFON And this one here, is he having fun? °
    Look how I get to work.

GESTAS Ah, cursed be the day and the hour
    that God had me born into the world!   26,456
    I would not be here

26,423–66 John 19:32

26,449 *Il a bien des poires d'angoisse.* A pun: Angoisse is a village in Dordogne and means "anguish" (Rychner and Henry, *Le Testament Villon*, II, 111).

26,453 *pelle il chastaigne.* A proverbial phrase (Hassell, 67).

if this miserable Jesus
had wanted to show his might.
But no, his sense has failed   26,460
and has let him and us die
a shameful and wretched death.
GRIFFON Your carcass is given over to death.
    You're wasting your time in bawling so loudly.   26,464
ORILLART They're both dead, more or less.
    They're gasping for their last breath.
MICHAEL I would like to bring this soul
    to the place of luminous glory   26,468
    where the gentle Jesus has brought
    his friends to comfort them.
SATAN And this one, I would like to carry
    to the place of thunderous rage,   26,472
    where the devil is determined
    to torment his lackeys.

> *Here St. Michael takes the good thief to the place where
> the prophets are, and Satan takes the bad thief to hell*

BROYEFORT Come on soldiers, we must hurry up.
    Since these two bad thieves   26,476
    are disposed of, we'll leave them
    and go murder this Jesus.
CLAQUEDENT I agree.
BRAYART And I'm in favor of it, too.
    Here's my great double edged axe   26,480
    which is keen and sharp.
    I'll crush him immediately.
GRIFFON Our mission is thwarted.
BRAYART What do you mean?
    You look like you've seen a ghost.   26,484
GRIFFON Jesus is dead. Look.
    His soul has left his body.
BROYEFORT We'd really be foolish
    to break his bones or joints.   26,488
    Let's leave him to chance.
    Since he's dead, that's enough for us.
LONGINUS When alive, he never harmed me,
    but nevertheless I do not lament   26,492
    that he now has passed away.
    Everyone says that his death is good,
    but it troubles my heart
    that I didn't get here before he died.   26,496

Nevertheless, since I came here,
I would like to make use of my means,
and if one of you guides me
and wishes to direct my lance,   26,500
he'll receive a blow, so he may die,
if he is not already dead at this hour.
ORILLART I'm all for it.
BRAYART Me too.
Come here, I'll direct you.   26,504
Push hard when I say so.
I'll put you within reach.
LONGINUS Am I correctly positioned?
BRAYART In the best place ever,
exactly on the right side.   26,508
LONGINUS That's just where I want to be.
You've not chosen the spot badly.
Now then enter, by God!
If he's alive, I'm afraid he'll feel it.   26,512
BROYEFORT You've given him quite a gash,
the blood flows beyond measure
all along your lance.
Such a stroke is formidable.   26,516
LONGINUS How can a dead man bleed?
I hold it a great marvel.
GRIFFON The lance is all red,
so abundantly has it flowed.   26,520
CENTURION There is not only blood °
but with the blood, clear water,
which signifies some mystery
of which we have no knowledge.   26,524
And it truly seems to me
that this Jesus who is dead
is unjustly and wrongly
condemned to such shame.   26,528
No one is so stupid as not to see this.
The signs clearly testified to it.
I judged him to be the true son of God
and said and still say   26,532
that the noble king of paradise
shows these signs here for his sake.
My people, depart from here.

26,521–24 John 19:34.

When I look at Jesus and these two,   26,536
    there's no longer need for a guard.
    They are all dead of a cruel death.
RUBION Let's go report the news
    to Pilate, our procurator.   26,540
ASCANIUS Unless he hears it soon,
    he'll worry greatly.

Here they go to Pilate

LONGINUS O Jesus, I beg your mercy   26,544
    for the harm I did you.
    Never did I think
    you were such a noble person
    as the Centurion proposes.
    You are gentle and full of clemency,   26,548
    and in this trust
    I will take and put on my eyes
    the pure blood flowing from you,
    the dear and precious drop,   26,552
    hoping that it makes me better
    and that my sight is restored.
    O Jesus, the truth and the way
    and the salvation which never goes astray   26,556
    in order to enlighten all sinners,
    reason demands that I should praise you,
    for a moment ago I did not see at all.
    Now you have given me grace   26,560
    and poured out your pity on me
    by returning and restoring to me
    my missing sight.
BROYEFORT Our work is done.   26,564
    Comrades, let's think of returning.

Here the citizens return to Pilate

JOSEPH OF ARIMATHEA Charity and perfect love °
    cannot be held enclosed,
    but must be freed   26,568
    and sweetly surrendered
    to the one to whom they are given.

26,566–27,053 Matthew 27:57–58; Mark 15:42–43; Luke 23:50–52; John 19:38–42;
Passion d'Arras (lines 18,277–496). In John 19:38 Joseph of Arimathea is a disciple
in secret. In the *Passion d'Arras*, Joseph goes with Nicodemus to Pilate.

I say this because
I loyally and secretly served   26,572
gentle Jesus during his life.
Therefore I won't forsake him after his death,
but will continue to serve
his sweet and most holy countenance   26,576
to show that I am his servant.

Here he comes before Pilate and says

Sir procurator, may God give you joy,
and may your honor be upheld!
PILATE You are welcome here,   26,580
sir Joseph of Arimathea.
What brings you to these parts
now so quickly?
JOSEPH OF ARIMATHEA The dreadful awe   26,584
of the signs that appeared
at the moment of Jesus' death,
which everyone fears and marvels at,
brings me before you, dear sir,   26,588
to obtain a request.
PILATE Joseph, it's necessary to conclude
that the affair was badly conducted,
although I must be acquitted of this.   26,592
I am not guilty of anything.
The envious Jews,
who made me judge
by force and violence,   26,596
did this to satisfy their arrogance.
JOSEPH OF ARIMATHEA In regard to the excuse
I make no argument as to whether
he died rightly or wrongly.   26,600
God, the just judge, knows all.
PILATE That's true.
JOSEPH OF ARIMATHEA For this, my lord,
to pacify the people,
I come here to beseech you   26,604
that a great favor may be granted me,
that the body of this prophet
be given and returned to me.
It will be taken down by me   26,608
for the honor of human nature,
and then put in its sepulchre
as ordered by the law.

PILATE Joseph, you do well to ask.   26,612
    Because of your honor,
    I grant you your petition.
    Go and remove it right away.
JOSEPH OF ARIMATHEA I thank you, sir procurator.   26,616
    I will immediately hurry.
    May God grant that I work well!
    Never have I been granted a request
    at which my heart felt such joy.   26,620
    What more good can I ask?
NICODEMUS Joseph, may God protect you from °
    shame and evil blasphemy!
JOSEPH OF ARIMATHEA You are welcomed, Nicodemus   26,624
    and received with great joy!
    I think God brings you here
    to guide me in this matter.
NICODEMUS How are you? What do you have to do   26,628
    that you go so quickly?
JOSEPH OF ARIMATHEA I'm returning from the procurator, Pilate,
    from whom I have obtained
    permission to retrieve Jesus' body,   26,632
    and if you don't mind waiting a bit,
    you can help me take it down,
    for I won't be able to do it alone.
NICODEMUS I feel great joy at this news,   26,636
    because I was secretly his poor disciple
    for many a winter and many a summer.
    Therefore I am happy
    if I can do him any service   26,640
    that would be good and pleasing to him.
JOSEPH OF ARIMATHEA Let us find the right way
    of doing this.
NICODEMUS We must first know   26,644
    where we can bury him.
JOSEPH OF ARIMATHEA Don't worry about that. °
    I have a very pretty garden
    close enough to where he is,   26,648
    in which not long ago I had
    a lovely tomb built

26,622 The source for Nicodemus' involvement in the burial of Christ is John 19:39.

26,646 John 19:41. In Matthew 27:60, the tomb belongs to Joseph of Arimathea.

for myself and my good friends.
Nevertheless, no one has yet been put in it.   26,652
If he is put there, he will be the first.
NICODEMUS If you believe me, we should hurry
to put him there with ceremony.
JOSEPH Explain, then.   26,656
NICODEMUS Here's how.
To shroud the holy body,
Joseph, you will seek
a sheet or a fine cloth,
the best that can be bought.   26,660
It will be used to enfold him.
In the meantime I will be busy
until I find a place
having the most precious unguents   26,664
that money can buy.
JOSEPH OF ARIMATHEA Bring a great abundance of them
to provide richly for the burial.
NICODEMUS Let me take care of it.   26,668
Whatever it might cost me,
I plan to bring so large a quantity
that it will amply suffice.
THE SILK MERCHANT I think that it's time   26,672
to display my merchandise.
I have cloth of many kinds,
winding-sheets and sendal,
silks, white and red satins,   26,676
beautiful and pleasing to look at.
JOSEPH Lady, may our great God protect you
and increase your fortune and honor!
THE MERCHANT Welcome noble lord!   26,680
Do you need anything that I have today?
Do you want fine sendal or silk
or some other fine merchandise?
Here is a cloth so well-woven   26,684
that there exists no better.
JOSEPH Here is what suits me.
How much will the winding-sheet cost?
THE MERCHANT Certainly my lord, it costs   26,688
six *besants* of ready cash. °
JOSEPH That's a lot.

26,689 *besant*. A Byzantine gold or silver coin.

THE MERCHANT It will have to cost that
    or I'll be giving it to you as a precious gift.
    But if it's not beautiful and suitable,   26,692
    you can return it for the price.
JOSEPH Since you will not lower the price,
    here is your money, all counted out.
THE MERCHANT I pray to the king of majesty   26,696
    that he grant you joy in its use.
    You cannot be cheated.
    The merchandise is flawless and perfect.
NICODEMUS If you have costly essences   26,700
    in the form of excellent unguents,
    fragrant and redolent,
    I beg you, master spice vendor,
    that my desire be fulfilled   26,704
    and that you will show me many of them.
THE SPICE MERCHANT First, I must know
    which kind you prefer.
NICODEMUS I want myrrh and aloes °   26,708
    mixed in an appropriate unguent
    about eighty or a hundred pounds,
    according to what price is given me.
THE SPICE MERCHANT Whoever buys in great quantity   26,712
    rightfully gets a better price.
    Is this what you need?
    The unguent is of great worth.
NICODEMUS I ask for only the best,   26,716
    and I will give what it's worth.
THE SPICE MERCHANT Here, this is the amount you need.
    At no price could anyone have
    a better unguent than   26,720
    the one I'm giving you.
NICODEMUS How much will it all cost?
THE SPICE MERCHANT Don't worry about it,
    my lord. I know you well.
    I can't lose anything with you.   26,724
    I see by your busy expression
    that your work is urgent.

26,708–11 In John 19:39, Nicodemus brings about a hundred pounds of myrrh and
aloes. Gréban depicts Nicodemus as a generous man who meets a kind merchant,
while Joseph of Arimathea, concerned about the price of silk, encounters a more
business-minded merchant. This scene is not in Marcadé.

Go to where your business is,
and we will always be in agreement   26,728
concerning the price.
NICODEMUS Therefore, I will return to in haste.
Master, may the great God favor you!
From what I can make out   26,732
I see that Joseph has returned,
having finished his part,
and is only waiting for me.
Sir Joseph, as I observe,   26,736
you show great diligence.
JOSEPH OF ARIMATHEA Nicodemus, we must begin
at once making preparations.
The ladder is all ready;   26,740
here are iron pliers and hammers.
NICODEMUS The arms of the cross are very high.
We cannot reach it any other way.
JOSEPH Let's not hold back. °   26,744
With all my strength I'm going to
pull out those great nails.
Place yourself a little lower.
When I've taken the nail out of one arm,   26,748
you must hold firmly
and support this noble body,
so that it does not fall to the ground.
NICODEMUS You needn't say more.   26,752
I'll be very careful.
JOSEPH OF ARIMATHEA This nail is not easy to remove.
I don't know who drove it in so well.
NICODEMUS Joseph, from what I can see,   26,756
this nail is not easy to remove.
JOSEPH May whoever hammered it in so deeply
have a cold night!
NICODEMUS This nail is not easy to remove.   26,760
JOSEPH OF ARIMATHEA I don't know who drove it in so well.
Finally, I got one of them out,
but here's one that clings just as tightly.
NICODEMUS It cannot be unfastened so quickly.   26,764
JOSEPH OF ARIMATHEA Finally, I got one of them out.

26,744 Both Marcadé and Gréban reverse the action described in *Meditations on the Life of Christ* (341), where Joseph holds Christ's body while Nicodemus removes the nails.

NICODEMUS If the other one were taken out,
  he would no longer hang by the hands.
JOSEPH OF ARIMATHEA Finally, I got one of them out,   26,768
  but here's one that clings just as tightly.
NICODEMUS Pull hard there.
JOSEPH OF ARIMATHEA I'm not hesitating,
  but you, support him in front.
NICODEMUS I regret that you're having trouble.   26,772
  Pull hard there!
JOSEPH OF ARIMATHEA I'm not hesitating.
  I think I've got it.
  Give me my hammer.
NICODEMUS Here.
  Pull hard there.   26,776
JOSEPH OF ARIMATHEA I'm not hesitating,
  but you, support him in front.
NICODEMUS I'm holding him. Now take care of
  his feet and then you'll be done.
JOSEPH OF ARIMATHEA I think it's holding tightly.   26,780
NICODEMUS Yes, it is.
  I think it's true,
  for the nail that's driven in here
  is horribly big and sharp.
JOSEPH OF ARIMATHEA I'll pull with such force   26,784
  that, before I'm done, I'll have it.
NICODEMUS O holy body, precious and worthy,
  you brought us many a great good!
JOSEPH OF ARIMATHEA O false Jews and wicked people,   26,788
  you have cruelly repaid him.
NICODEMUS All his life he strove,
  the very sweet and piteous Jesus,
  to give them aid and comfort.   26,792
JOSEPH OF ARIMATHEA Alas, now he is dearly sold,
  for they never stopped
  until they brought about his death.
  My heart torments me   26,796
  to hold you dead,
  honored, holy body
  that for our support,
  salvation and happiness   26,800
  worked so hard.
  Your noble soul was devoted
  and consecrated
  royally to God.   26,804

Now you are dead, O fruit of life,
because of envy
and unjust judgment.

NICODEMUS It cannot happen otherwise.   26,808
It is done. The decision is made.
Our lords have too much contempt.
Who would have dared oppose them?
But truly, we can indeed say   26,812
that no man born of a mother
was ever so terribly assailed
as he was before he died.

JOSEPH OF ARIMATHEA It's obvious; don't they see it?   26,816
His body carries the marks.

OUR LADY My sisters and my dear companions,
let us approach the cross.
I think I see there   26,820
Joseph and Nicodemus,
who, inspired by loyal love,
are taking down the body of my son.

SAINT JOHN My lady, it's true. They are there.   26,824
I speak as it seems to me.

MARY JACOBI We will go together towards them.
But if you believe me in this matter,
you will not come dear sister,   26,828
for when you see him taken down,
I am sure that you will feel
bitter and boundless grief
and cry such an abundance of tears   26,832
that your heart will break.

OUR LADY My sister, if it pleases God, it will not be so.
I will restrain myself with all my strength,
but not for anything will I refrain from   26,836
seeing my son taken down before my eyes,
my blood and my offspring,
my love, the best of my treasures,
whom I gently and tenderly nourished.   26,840
I want to know what will happen to him,
who will have him, who will secure him,
and in what place he shall be put
by his good and loyal friends.   26,844
God, his father, invited me
to be present at his nativity,
present at his circumcision,
and at his presentation   26,848

and worthy reception in the temple,
present at his public life
noted for love and perfect joy,
and present at his death. Alas,   26,852
what severe and violent torment
and piercing anguish does
the heart of a sad and mournful mother feel.
Therefore, may God never consent   26,856
that the frailty of nature
should prevent me from seeing his burial
and that I should not be present at it!

MARY SALOMÉ We must follow her immediately.   26,860
    She's going there without delaying any longer.
MAGDALENE Nothing would make her linger;
    natural love leads her.
JOSEPH OF ARIMATHEA Argh, did this nail hurt me!   26,684
    It was so deeply hammered in
    that sweat is running down my forehead
    from pulling it and from the hard work
    I undertook.   26,868
NICODEMUS Since it's out,
    the worst of my difficulties is over.
    Nothing remains except to take him down,
    which will be laborious enough.
JOSEPH OF ARIMATHEA Step down in front   26,872
    and support him on your side there
    with all your strength.
NICODEMUS I am striving
    with all my strength to do it,
    but also be certain of that side.   26,876
    Use all your force,
    it is certainly needed.
JOSEPH OF ARIMATHEA Have no fear.
    I will not be neglectful.
OUR LADY Ah, my child, ah, my love,   26,880
    ah, my treasure, ah, my wealth!
    Give me back the only possession
    that I will ever seek in the world.
    Alas, I humbly ask you   26,884
    that I have him with me
    and that I never cease
    kissing and holding him,
    until my heart feels satisfied   26,888
    and ever so slightly joyful.

Since I could not enjoy him
when he was alive as I would have wished,
since he was taken from me while alive   26,892
and violently ravished,
murdered without having deserved it,
at least let my very dear son
. after such a bitter death   26,896
be returned to his grieving mother.
JOSEPH OF ARIMATHEA We have waited a long time.
Lady, he must be shrouded.
We don't know who is coming or going.   26,900
Please cease your tears
and for the moment hold them back,
until he has been put into his tomb.

Holding him dead, Mary says

OUR LADY Jesus, my dear child, Jesus   26,904
my love, the sum total of my blessing,
I have no other blessing.
When alive you so pleased
your dear mother,   26,908
my good, my perfect light,
my last and first joy.
Alas, what countenance,
what disposition   26,912
does my heart full of affliction contain
when I have lost all my comfort,
my love, my son, my pleasure
whom I hold dead.   26,916
False Death
how did you have the audacity
to take only my son
without killing me also.   26,920
Cruelly,
falsely,
you behaved against me.
My child, my sweet offspring,   26,924
you leave me sorrowful,
and kept away,
thrust away,
from all good that can come to me.   26,928
Alas, my very dear remembrance,
once, at the time of your tender youth,
I was accustomed to holding you

~ 187 ~

on my lap, in great joy,
in desire,
in pleasure, 26,932
while gazing at your gracious appearance,
your humility,
your simplicity, 26,936
whose beauty was my treasure.
There I kissed you a thousand times;
with kissing I satisfied my heart.
I thought of you, 26,940
I watched over you
very carefully; God knows
no mother could do better.
Alas, king of the heavens, 26,944
these kisses are no longer such
because my eyes
see you dead of a shameful death,
of a terrible and painful death 26,948
and your holy, precious flesh
noble,
pitiful,
torn on all sides! 26,952

NICODEMUS My lady, for God's sake, listen.
You see that night approaches,
and these Jews, full of disgrace, 26,956
could very well trouble us;
for God's sake, let us hurry
to anoint this precious body.

OUR LADY My dear friends, I agree, 26,960
but God knows that I do so very reluctantly.
O, my son, where are the speeches,
the sweet words, the beautiful sayings
with which you once consoled me 26,964
and gave joy to my poor heart?
Alas, I could not enjoy
you when you lived in the world,
even though you were all mine. 26,968
No man could claim anything.
How bitter to me now that
after your death and this grievous sorrow
I cannot hold you at my will 26,972
to dispel my grave distress.

SAINT JOHN My lady and my dear mistress,
for God's sake, soothe your pains

and allow these good lords   26,976
to finish what they undertook.

Here they all together anoint him and then put him in his shroud °

MAGDALENE O my dear master of great worth,
    descended from the sovereign realm,
    the most perfect who ever ruled,   26,980
    how have you deserved this,
    that I see you deprived of life,
    for which my heart wishes to melt with tears?
    False Jews, may God destroy you!   26,984
    Think well on what you have done.
    Never was such a crime seen,
    never was there such envy,
    never was more mortal hatred   26,988
    shown to a creature.
    It was your perverse nature
    that never rested in peace
    until he suffered death,   26,992
    which he never deserved.
    For which in the end may you be served
    pain and terrible vengeance!
    This is my belief, this is my hope.   26,996
    I cannot believe
    that the infinite creator
    would leave such a crime unpunished.
JOSEPH OF ARIMATHEA Now lords, let us all occupy   27,000
    ourselves in finishing our work.
    The lavishly anointed body
    has been placed in its shroud.
NICODEMUS Let us bring him to the tomb   27,004
    gently, carefully;
    you lift him in front and I in the back,
    we'll soon put him there.
OUR LADY O my very dear and true friends,   27,008
    do not hasten me from
    my child, for I will die
    if I am far from his sweet face.

Stage direction after 26,977 In Luke 23:55–56, the women see the tomb and then
return to it on Sunday with spices and ointments. In Gréban they participate
immediately and directly in the burial, as they also do in *Meditations on the Life of
Christ* and in the *Passion d'Arras*.

MARY JACOBI Dear sister, it must be done.
      You only make it worse.
      For God's sake, let them finish.
      Their work has a most sacred significance.

   Here they bury him, and in the meanwhile Our Lady says

OUR LADY O true God and eternal father, °   27,016
      who made the sky and earth from nothing,
      why did you ever give me a son
      when I did not ask for him,
      when I remain on earth,   27,020
      devastated by such loss,
      losing you in such pain?
      O holy archangel Gabriel,
      O spiritual messenger   27,024
      of the sovereign realm,
      where is the pleasant joy
      that you promised me in your salutation?
      It seems that it was worth little to me.   27,028
      I find your promise poor
      when instead of gaiety I feel sadness,
      more than does any living woman,
      and my poor soul strives with   27,030
      death who does not want to take it.
JOSEPH OF ARIMATHEA He is so well positioned that, considering
         everything,
      one could not better place him.
NICODEMUS I hear your words gladly,   27,036
      but something is lacking in our work,
      for we have done nothing
      if we do not close the tomb.
JOSEPH OF ARIMATHEA We agree with your opinion.   27,040
      It is unnecessary to seek any closing
      other than this big stone;
      it will serve exactly.
SAINT JOHN You speak truly. However,
      it is extremely heavy.
NICODEMUS We have sufficient enough
      force to carry it there.
JOSEPH OF ARIMATHEA If each one of us puts himself into it,
      we'll succeed.   27,049

27,016–22 A complaint by the Virgin (Sinclair, 253).

Now, lift hard there!

SAINT JOHN Up!

NICODEMUS Up!
It's almost in place.
Never in my life   27,052
have I lifted such a big load.

SAINT JOHN It's in place.

JOSEPH OF ARIMATHEA It's placed well.
Our feat is accomplished,
and so we'll take leave of   27,056
these good and worthy women.

OUR LADY Prudent and wise people,
my lords full of knowledge,
we heartily thank you   27,060
for your good care.

MARY SALOMÉ Let us leave, dear sister,
you and these good holy women,
and cease your cries and lamentations   27,064
in the name of the noble creator.

OUR LADY O my son and my true teacher,
in whom my heart has its only refuge,
must I separate myself from you?   27,068
Alas, what bitter parting,
when she whom you regard as mother
leaves you pierced by death
and alone in your tomb.   27,072
I withdraw very reluctantly from this place.
I ask your father, who is God,
that I will soon hear news of you
and that shortly my heart will rejoice   27,076
in seeing your resurrection.

MAGDALENE Let us go to our home
my lady; this seems good to me,
and together there we will console ourselves   27,080
for our severe distress.

OUR LADY Devout lady Magdalene,
I completely and willingly agree.

CAIAPHAS Lords, I would like to call your attention to   27,084
a point which concerns the law.
Please come with me.
I would like to say right away two words
to Pilate, our governor,   27,088
that greatly bear on our case.

ELYACHIM We will not leave you,

but will follow you there and elsewhere.
BARRAQUIN What do these good lords demand,   27,092
   who come here in such haste?
CAIAPHAS Barraquin, is my lord Pilate
   very busy?
BARRAQUIN No, but he's in such a rotten mood,   27,096
   that he's almost pissing blood.
   He's glued to his seat
   where he's lost in his imagination.
   He's daydreaming so much   27,100
   that he hasn't stopped since noon.
   I don't know what the devil is wrong.
   He hasn't been so worked up in a long time.
ANNAS Could we talk to him?   27,104
   Only a few words. See if we can.
BARRAQUIN I doubt it very much and do not know,
   for he is really irritated,
   more than I am accustomed to,   27,108
   but I'll still perform my duty.
ISACAR Therefore, good sir, go find out
   if we can talk to him.
BARRAQUIN Dear sir, the Pharisees   27,112
   are here in great number.
PILATE Be quiet, good sir, I beg you.
   I have no interest in their coming.
   Cursed be Jupiter and Mercury   27,116
   that I ever got involved with them!
BARRAQUIN Argh, how cruel he is.
   One dare not say a word too soon.
   But even if he should foam with anger,   27,120
   I'll say what I must.
   My lord, should they enter
   or shall they be dismissed?
   They have waited enough out there.   27,124
   Turn your attention to that.
PILATE Are they still waiting there?
   I had already forgotten.
   I am so melancholic   27,128
   that I don't know what to do.
BARRAQUIN What will I say?
PILATE Have them come in.
   Let Jupiter rejoice about this!
BARRAQUIN Come lords, your places are ready.   27,132
   Enter. My lord orders it.

JEROBOAM We cause him much worry,
    but we will redress all in the end.
CAIAPHAS Dear sir, may the divine throne   27,136
    be your everlasting home!
    We again seek recourse
    in your honorable person,
    but, for God's sake, judge, let it not weigh upon you   27,140
    if you have trouble on our account.
PILATE Come to the point which brings you here.
    You've talked enough.
CAIAPHAS My lord, it is true °   27,144
    that in considering the affair of Jesus,
    who has been taken down from the cross,
    we remembered all of a sudden
    how during his life he said   27,148
    that he would be resuscitated in three days
    from the hour of his death,
    which causes us great worry.
PILATE And so, even if that were the case,   27,152
    what do you want done about it?
CAIAPHAS If it pleases you, by your grace,
    obtain proven knights,
    the most courageous you have,   27,156
    who will guard the tomb
    carefully and well.
    We are happy to pay
    each of them his wages,   27,160
    as long as he does his duty well.
PILATE As for me, I don't understand anything.
    For what reason do you think of this?
ANNAS Dear sir, there is reason enough.   27,164
    I understand our master, I think.
    He fears, and so do I,
    lest the disciples of that man,
    whom he assembled and gathered   27,168
    in great number, with some malice,
    come by night in the darkness,
    take him, and steal him from us,
    and then by common consent,   27,172

27,144–265 Matthew 27:62–66. The guarding of the tomb occurs in the Fourth Day of the *Passion d'Arras* (lines 20,100–299). Marcadé's Third Day ends with the Deposition.

tell and preach to the people
that he is resuscitated from death,
which will cause us great embarrassment.
CAIAPHAS He's right. They are numberless.   27,176
Death, to which we have submitted him,
will not have served us anything,
but this killing will turn
to our confusion,   27,180
and this last error will be
much worse than the first,
for everyone would believe in him
and in believing would abandon us   27,184
and all our jurisdiction.
PILATE Since you have such great fear
of his disciples assembling together,
coming by night, or stealing him   27,188
by malice as you think,
you will have enough guards.
Take three of the most
skilled and the swiftest   27,192
of our knights,
who will take care of it.
CENTURION If you wish to believe my expertise
and give fair wages,
enough so that my people are happy,   27,196
I have three proven knights,
bold and valiant men,
who especially seek such conflicts
and who were in many great armies   27,200
in which they conducted themselves nobly.
JORAM By your grace, lend them to us,
worthy lord Centurion;
all together we beg you,   27,204
and we will pay them high wages.
CENTURION Don't tell me such things
just to trick my comrades.
MARDOCEE Whatever happens, we will respond by   27,208
compensating them fully.
CENTURION Then, you will have them immediately.
Now come here, Ascanius,
Marcus Antonius, and Emilius.   27,212
You hear these good lords
begging you to guard
the tomb where Jesus lies.

〜 194 〜

Only three days are needed. 27,216
Let no one in the world take him,
and guard him so well that you can give him back to them
in the tomb at the end of three days.
ASCANIUS We will stay there so diligently 27,220
and keep such continual watch
that they will hear good news,
even if we must stand guard night and day.
RUBION We must prepare our equipment ° 27,224
and buckle our cuirasses well.
Let's get our coats of mail and our axes,
and we'll set out immediately.
EMILIUS We're so well suited up 27,228
that we lack no piece of armor.
Let's go, come what may,
to the place and see what happens.
ASCANIUS Jewish lords, there's one point 27,232
that I've thought of here.
if the body has already been removed
or stolen at this hour,
the blame would fall on us; 27,236
yet, there's nothing we could do.
CAIAPHAS Don't ever fear that.
We'll go with you step by step
and give you the body 27,240
actually in its tomb.
Then we'll all mark the grave
with our seals,
so that there cannot be any deception 27,244
for you or for us.
RUBION This is sensibly said.
Then let us now leave.

Here the Pharisees go with the knights to the tomb, and then Annas says

ANNAS We have come at the right time. 27,248
We need not fear any longer,
for here is the whole corpse
and the tomb well-closed.
CAIAPHAS Now it must be confirmed 27,252

---

after 27,223 Mark Anthony is here replaced by Rubion and does not return until
the action of the Fourth Day, when he also guards the tomb of Christ. The error
is probably scribal. In manuscripts A and D Mark Anthony does indeed appear
here as he should, since the Centurion has just called him to duty.

with seals and signatures,
so that at least nothing is stolen,
for we do not know what can happen.
Let each one make his own mark,   27,256
and let us leave these good lords here.

[Caiaphas affixes a great seal of red wax.]

JOATHAN I am satisfied.
ISACAR So am I.
I put my seal here.
JEROBOAM I think the stone is well sealed.   27,260
I believe he will not come out
without our knowing something about it.
We can now leave them here.
CAIAPHAS Lords, we leave you here   27,264
and commend you to God.

Here the Pharisees return to their places

ASCANIUS Now, my children, let's make sure
that no one can reproach us.
RUBION If there is a villain who approaches,   27,268
whether disciple or hypocrite,
I'll give him such a blow
that the devil will carry him away.
EMILIUS We'll see who will be courageous   27,272
and who will carry the banner.
You keep watch in front and I'll do so in the back.
The moon shines and the night is ready.
ASCANIUS Let whoever wants one on his head   27,276
come here! I challenge anyone.

FINAL PROLOGUE Lords and worthy people,
who have behaved like
people of noteworthy wisdom   27,280
and who have, without any weariness,
heard the timely deed
of the perfect obedience
which Jesus had in the presence   27,284
of his Father when he suffered death,
take example in the patience
with which for our offense
he offered his precious flesh.   27,288
Here we will end the Passion,
which with great effort
we have played before you.

On Sunday, we have the intention 27,292
of playing before you
the part about his Resurrection.
Let us pray to the honored Virgin
that she may show us 27,296
in the blessed region
the worthy and glorious face
of her son.

The End of the Third Day of the Passion of Our Lord Jesus Christ

Appendix

The following two extracts are intended to provide the reader with an opportunity to compare the translation with the language of the original text.

I. From the Prologue to the Third Day.

Pour continuer la matiere
qui est prouffitable et entiere
a cueurs plains de compassion,   19,908
laquelle traicte par maniere
la haulte passion planiere
qui fit nostre redempcion,
pour la nostre salvacion,   19,912
avant nostre incoacion,
chascun de nous saluera
la Vierge en contemplacion
et dirons par devocion   19,916
humblement *Ave Maria*.

Ave Maria

Ce devost salu accomply,
seigneurs, humblement je vous supply
que ung peu de scilence prestez   19,920
et l'entendement aprestez
a incorporer la doulceur,
charité et parfaicte amour
ou ceste passion admainne   19,924
et joinct toute nature humaine.
Penssez que celluy qui s'instruit
en ce livre porte grant fruit,

et qu'il n'est hystoire en ce monde   19,928
si fertille ne si feconde
ne qui doye mieulx faire entendre
le cueur au bien ou il doit tendre.
Qui bien l'escoute et bien l'entend,   19,932
a nul mal faire ne pretend,
mais juge tout plaisir mondain
mauvais, decepvable et soubdain,
et n'est adversité si forte   19,936
que tout pacïanment ne porte.
Car, quant en memoire luy vient
la fortune qui luy seurvient,
aucunement se desmodere,   19,940
mais aprés, quant il considere
que le filz de Dieu beneuré
a tant souffert et enduré
pour mondifier nostre ordure,   19,944
il treuve que ce qu'il endure
n'est riens au regard de la somme
que Jhesus voult porter pour l'omme.
Ainsi va ses dueulz moderant,   19,948
en ce mirouer considerant,
ou tout cueur, pour son dueil mirer,
se doit parfondement mirer.
Et, affin que vous y mirez   19,952
et doulcement la remirez,
ce devost mirouer pour le mieulx
vous ramenons devant les yeulx,
senssiblement, par parsonnaiges.   19,956
Mirez vous si serez bien saiges,
chascun sa fourme y entrevoit:
qui bien se mire bien se voit.
Dieu doint que si bien nous mirons   19,960
que, par mirer, nous remirons,
aprés ceste vie mortelle,
la puissant essence inmortelle
qui regne sans jamais tarir.   19,964

II. Judas laments having sold Christ.

Voyla mon maistre qu'on enmaine
assez piteusement traictié
et m'est advis que son traictié
piteusement se chevira   21,080

et que la mort s'en enssuivra:
il n'y a remedde en son fait.
O mauvais murtrier, qu'as tu fait?
Cueur desloyal, qu'as tu pensé? 21,084
Que t'es tu meffait?
Qu'as tu offenssé?
Tu as commancé
ung si grant meffait 21,088
que jamais n'en seras reffait
ne l'innocent recompenssé.
Par mon mauvais cueur et terrible
qu'oncques bien ne voult concevoir, 21,092
j'ay fait l'offense plus horrible
que jamais oeul peust percevoir.
Le juste innocent et paisible
ay fait par fraude decevoir 21,096
et cuide qu'il ne m'est possible
de jamais pardon recevoir.
Saint homme juste et diligent,
Jhesus ou tous biens sont compris, 21,100
je fus de ta gent
jadis et me pris;
et or, pour ung pris
de meschant argent, 21,104
mon pervers cueur et negligent
t'a vendu: c'est par trop mespris.
Maudicte et perverse peccune,
quel bouche assez te maudira! 21,108
Cause de dueil et de rancune
et en qui tant de maudire a!
Maudit soit le serf de Fortune
qui de la terre te tira, 21,112
quant, par toy, tel dueil me fortune
qui jamais ne me partira!
O maistre de vraye doctrine,
jadis en ton escolle fus: 21,116
haulte discipline,
non pas de reffuz.
Mal y entrefus,
je n'en suis pas digne 21,120
quand, par may traÿson maligne,
je m'en pars tristes et conffus.
Haa, chault brasier de convoitise
plus ardans que brandons de fer, 21,124

qui cueurs humains brase et atise
d'estincelles du feu d'enffer,
de quelle ardeur as tu esprise
ma voulenté pour l'enverser!   21,128
Tu m'as adressé la pourprise
d'enffer pour sans fin converser.
J'ay orreur de toy pocesser,
faulse peccune miserable;   21,132
tu m'as fait faire euvre du dyable
dont jamais quicte ne seray.
Pour tant je te repporteray
a ceulx qui de toy me douerent   21,136
et qui les motifz me donnerent
dont condempné me trouveray.

Bibliography

Accarie, Maurice. *Le Théâtre sacré de la fin du Moyen Age: Étude sur le sens moral de la 'Passion' de Jean Michel*. Geneva: Droz, 1979.

Aquinas, Thomas. *Summa Theologica*. Trans. Fathers of the English Dominican Province. 20 vols. London: Washbourne, 1911–25.

Aristotle. *Physique*. Trans. Henri Carteron. Paris: Les Belles Lettres, 1990.

Champion, Pierre. *Histoire poétique du quinzième siècle*. Paris: Vol. 2. Champion, 1923.

Chardon, Henri. *Les Gréban et les mystères dans le Maine*. Paris: Champion, 1879.

Chatelain, Henri. *Recherches sur le vers français au XVème siècle*. 1908; rpt. Geneva: Slatkine Reprints, 1974.

Crist, Larry S. "La Chute de l'homme sur la scène dans la France du XIIe et du XVe siècle." *Romania* 9 (1978): 207–19.

Cohen, Gustave. *Études d'histoire du théâtre en France au Moyen Age et à la Renaissance*. Paris: Gallimard, 1956.

———. *Histoire de la mise en scène dans le théâtre religieux français du Moyen Age*. 2d ed. Paris: Champion, 1951.

———, ed. *Le livre de conduite du régisseur et le compte y des dépenses pour le Mystère de la Passion joué à Mons en 1501*. Paris: Champion, 1925.

———, trans. *Mystère de la Passion des théophiliens: Adaptation littéraire de Gustave Cohen d'après Arnoul Greban et Jean Michel*. Paris: Richard Masse, 1950.

———. "Le Vocabulaire de la scénologie médiévale." *Zeitschrift für französische Sprache und Literatur* 66 (1956): 15–21.

Di Stefano, Giuseppe. *Dictionnaire des locutions en moyen français*. Montreal: CERES, 1991.

DuBruck, Edelgard. "The *Passion Isabeau* (1398) and Its Relationship to Fifteenth Century *mystères de la passion*." *Romania* 107 (1986): 77–91.

Enders, Jody May. "Rhetoric and the Origins of Drama in Arnoul

Gréban's 'Mystère de la Passion.'" Ph.D diss., Univ. of Pennsylvania, 1986.

L'Évangile de Nicodème: les versions courtes en ancien français et en prose. Ed. Alvin E. Ford. Geneva: Droz, 1973.

Flanigan, C. Clifford. "Comparative Literature and the Study of Medieval Drama." *Yearbook of Comparative and General Literature*, 35 (1986), 56–104.

Foxton, Cynthia. "Hell and the Devil in the Medieval French Drama: Vision of Damnation or Hope for Salvation?" *Dies Illa: Death in the Middle Ages: Proceedings of the 1983 Manchester Colloquium.* Ed. Jane H. M. Taylor, 71–79. Liverpool: Cairns, 1984.

Frank, Grace. *The Medieval French Drama.* Oxford: Clarendon Press, 1954.

Geufroi de Paris. *La Passion des Jongleurs.* Ed. Anne Joubert Amari Perry. Paris: Beauchesne, 1981.

Gompertz, Stéphane. "La Justice et l'écriture: transcendence et soumission dans *Le mystère de la Passion* d'Arnoul Gréban." *La Licorne* 1 (1976): 73–93.

Gréban, Arnoul. *Le "Mystère de la Passion" d'Arnoul Gréban.* Ed. Omer Jodogne. 2 vols. Brussels: Palais des Académies, 1965–1983.

———. *Le Mystère de la Passion d'Arnould Greban.* Ed. Gaston Paris and Gaston Raynaud. Paris: Vieweg, 1878.

———. *Le Mystère de la Passion.* Trans. Micheline de Combarieu du Grès and Jean Subrenat. Paris: Gallimard, 1987.

———. *Le vray mistère de la passion d'Arnoul Gréban.* Trans. Charles Gailly de Taurines and Léonel de la Tourrasse. Bayonne: Édition Arts Graphiques, 1936.

———. *The Nativity.* Trans. Shelley Sewall. Carbondale: Southern Illinois Univ. Press, 1991.

Hamilton, Edith. *Mythology.* Boston: Little, Brown, 1942.

Hassell, James Woodrow. *Middle French Proverbs, Sentences, and Proverbial Phrases.* Toronto: Pontifical Institute of Mediaeval Studies, 1982.

Jacobus de Voragine. *The Golden Legend.* Trans. Granger Ryan and Helmut Ripperger. 2 vols. London: Longmans, Green, 1941.

Jodogne, Omer. "Le Souci du peuple dans les mystères français." *Les Études Classiques* 37 (1969): 338–50.

———. "La Structure des mystères français." *Revue Belge de Philologie et d'Histoire* 42 (1964): 827–42.

———. "Le Théâtre français du moyen âge: recherches sur l'aspect dramatique des textes." In *The Medieval Drama,* ed. Sandro Sticca, 1–21. Albany: State Univ. of New York Press, 1972.

———. "Le Théâtre médiéval et sa transmission par le livre." *Research Studies* 32 (1964): 63–75.

Kirkup, James, trans. *The True Mistery of the Passion: Adapted and Trans-*

lated from the French Medieval Mystery Cycle of Arnoul and Simon Gréban. London: Oxford University Press, 1962.

Knight, Alan E. Aspects of Genre in Late Medieval French Drama. Manchester: Manchester Univ. Press, 1983.

Kolve, V. A. The Play Called Corpus Christi. Stanford: Stanford Univ. Press, 1966.

Konigson, Elie. L'Espace théâtral médiéval. Paris: Centre National de la Recherche Scientifique, 1975.

Lebègue, Raymond. "La Passion d'Arnoul Gréban." Romania 60 (1934): 218–31.

Lièvre, Pierre. "Le vray mistère de la Passion d'Arnoul Gréban." Mercure de France 264 (1935): 364–68.

Lubac, Henri de. Exégèse médiévale: les quatre sens de l'Écriture. Vol. 4. Paris: Aubier, 1964.

Marcadé, Eustache. Le Mystère de la Passion: Texte du manuscrit 697 de la Bibliothèque d'Arras. Ed. Jules-Marie Richard. 1891; rpt. Geneva: Slatkine Reprints, 1976.

Michel, Jean. Le Mystère de la Passion (Angers 1486). Ed. Omer Jodogne. Gembloux: Duculot, 1959.

Le Mystère de la Passion de Troyes. Ed. Jean-Claude Bibelot. 2 vols. Geneva: Droz, 1987.

Le Mystère de la Passion Nostre Seigneur. Ed. Graham A. Runnalls. Geneva: Droz, 1974.

La Passion d'Autun. Ed. Grace Frank. Paris: Société des Anciens Textes Français, 1934.

La Passion d'Auvergne. Ed. Graham A. Runnalls. Geneva: Droz, 1982.

The "Passion de Semur." Ed. Peter Durbin and Lynette Muir. Leeds: Centre for Medieval Studies, 1981.

La Passion du Palatinus: mystère du XIVe siècle. Ed. Grace Frank. Paris: Champion, 1922.

La Passion Isabeau: une édition du manuscrit Fr. 966 de la Bibliothèque Nationale de Paris. Ed. Edelgard DuBruck. New York: Peter Lang, 1990.

Petit de Julleville, Louis. Histoire du théâtre en France: Les mystères. 2 vols. 1880; rpt. Geneva: Slatkine Reprints, 1968.

Piolin, Paul. Le théâtre chrétien dans le Maine au cours du Moyen Age. Mamers: Fleury et Dangin, 1891.

Porter, Lambert. La fatrasie et le fatras: Essai sur la poésie irrationnelle en France au Moyen Age. Geneva: Droz, 1960.

Potter, Robert. "Translation, Transplantation, Exfoliation: A Liberation Theology for Medieval Drama." Division of Medieval and Renaissance Drama Society, MLA Convention, New York, 28 Dec. 1986.

Pseudo-Bonaventura. Meditations on the Life of Christ: An Illustrated Manuscript of the Fourteenth Century (Paris, Bibliothèque Nationale, *ms. ital. 115)*. Trans. Isa Ragusa and Rosalie B. Green. Princeton: Princeton Univ. Press, 1961.

Rey-Flaud, Henri. *Le Cercle magique: Essai sur le théâtre en rond à la fin du Moyen Age*. Paris: Gallimard, 1973.

Roques, Gilles. Rev. of Arnoul Gréban, *Le mystère de la Passion*, ed. Omer Jodogne. *Revue de Linguistique Romane*, 47 (1983), 511–14.

Roy, Émile. *Le Mystère de la Passion en France du XIVe au XVIe siècle*. 1903; repr. Geneva: Slatkine Reprints, 1974.

Ruelle, Pierre. Review of *Le Mystère de la Passion*, by Arnoul Gréban, ed. Omer Jodogne. *Romania* 104 (1983): 589–91.

Runnalls, Graham A. Review of *Le Mystère de la Passion*, by Arnoul Gréban, trans. Micheline de Combarieu du Grès and Jean Subrenat. *French Studies*, 43 (1989), 76–77.

———. "Quatre fragments de manuscrits de mystères de la Passion." *Miscellanea Gasca Queirazza* 2 (1988): 911–18.

Sinclair, Keith. *French Devotional Texts of the Middle Ages: A Bibliographic Manuscript Guide*. Second Supplement. New York: Greenwood Press, 1988.

Stein, Henri. "Arnoul Gréban, poète et musicien." *Bibliothèque de l'École des Chartes* 79 (1918): 142–46.

Snyder, Susan Brooke. "The Paradox of Despair: Studies of the Despair Theme in Medieval and Renaissance Literature." Ph.D diss., Columbia Univ., 1963.

Sticca, Sandro. *The Planctus Mariae in the Dramatic Tradition of the Middle Ages*. Trans. Joseph R. Berrigan. Athens: Univ. of Georgia Press, 1988.

Stratman, Carl J. *Bibliography of Medieval Drama*. 2d ed. New York: Ungar, 1972.

Thiry, Claude. "Une Avocate inspirée? Procula dans quelques passions françaises." *Le Moyen Français* 11 (1982): 54–88.

Traver, Hope. *The Four Daughters of God: A Study of the Versions of this Allegory with Special Reference to Those in Latin, French, and English*. Bryn Mawr, Pa.: Bryn Mawr College, 1907.

Wadsworth, Randolph L. "The Bourreaux in Arnoul Gréban's *Mystère de la Passion*." *Revue de Littérature Comparée* 44 (1970): 499–509.

Warren, Glenda. "Les diables dans la *Passion* d'Arnoul Gréban." *Chimères: A Journal of French and Italian Literature* 15 (1981): 9–26.